THE HUNGRY RENEGADE

A cookbook for the damned – hold the garnish

a

Memoir

by László Szűcs

Rendered duck fat, thick in the air, coating the lungs like a second skin. A squeeze of lemon zest cuts through it—sharp, bright, momentary—before it's swallowed whole by the deeper perfume of shallots sweating down in butter. A leg of lamb spits and crackles on the flat-top, a golden crust forming where flesh meets steel, while a sauté pan flares up in the corner, a blaze roaring toward the ceiling.

"Behind!" someone shouts. A body brushes past, barely missing me with a smoking-hot pan.

This isn't a kitchen. It's a fucking furnace. A slaughterhouse with better lighting. The air is heavy—service is in full swing, the expeditor's barking like he's storming Normandy, the grill guy's drowning in tickets, and the dishwasher's wearing that thousand-yard stare you only get from a full sink and no end in sight. The fryer station smells like a heart attack, the pastry chef's cursing in French. And somewhere behind me, a rookie just burned his palm because he forgot the golden rule—pans don't have handles in the middle of service.

This is what it is to cook for a living. It's not about art, or passion, or any of that Michelin-starred bullshit people love to romanticize. It's about survival. And not everyone survives. Cooks disappear mid-service. Some storm out in a fit. Others just go out for a smoke and never return. The pressure crushes them. Weak ones wash out—ghosts before their aprons even hit the floor. The ones who stay? They're a special breed. Maniacs. Guys who like impossible. The ones who don't just survive the anarchy—they thrive in it. The ones who see the flames licking at their fingers and lean in closer.

Me? I wouldn't change it for anything. I wasn't supposed to be here. A Communist-bloc kid from Hungary with a bad attitude and a knack for pissing off authority, I should've ended up stuck in some state-run factory, assembling refrigerators for a government that didn't believe in cold beer. Instead, I smuggled my way

into kitchens across Africa and America—dodging immigration officers, and threading my way through places where yelling was the house language.

I spent three years cooking on cruise ships. Learned to make gefilte fish for a London power broker. Ran a grill for a South African gold miner who paid in cash and safari trips. Became sous chef at one of England's oldest haunted pubs—where the ghosts were the least of my concerns. And once, in Los Angeles, I plated Foie Gras for a man who introduced himself as "the guy who fixes problems for billionaires", drank slivovitz like water, and tipped in war stories.

And after all that? I'm just a guy with a set of knives and two kids to feed. Because here's the dirty secret they never tell you: There's no fucking money in cooking.

This is that story.

Pannónia Nyomda Kft.

Budapest 2025

László Szűcs

THE HUNGRY RENEGADE

A cookbook for the damned – hold the garnish

a

Memoir

Pannónia Nyomda Kft.

Budapest 2025

Contents

1. Shoulder It 1
2. A Rebel in the Gray 6
3. Beaten with Love (and a Backhand) 11
4. The Basement of Blood 17
5. Blood-Red Gold 23
6. Pharaohs Don't Do Room Service 28
7. The Black Bridge Inn 33
8. Kitchen Hopper, California Dreamin' 40
9. Angel from Hungary 46
10. Syrah, Sunburn, and the Goddess in Flip-Flops 50
11. Kitchen Legend 53
12. The Road Through El Paso 57
13. The Art of the Hopper 65
14. LA RAW 72
15. The Culinary Crossroads 76
16. The FBI, and a One-Way Ticket Out 82
17. Escape from California, Straight into the Fire 86
18. The Journey South 98
19. The Last Wait 105
20. A Dream on the Rocks – Malta 108
21. Smoke, Bees, and Burnt Wood 115
22. Back to the Steel Beast 121
23. The Ship Eats Its Own 131
24. The Staircase and the Lobster Rebellion 141
25. Champagne and Camouflage 146
26. Portugal or Bust – The €6,000 Gamble 152
27. Welcome to England (Now Duck) 158
28. The Lion, the Lobster, and the Leash 162
29. Exit File for the Next Chef (Classified) 165
30. Field Notes from KwaZulu-Natal 169
31. Fish Bones and Stolen Statues 179
32. Absence in White Gloves 183
33. The Other Knife in the Kitchen 191
34. Peacehaven – The Town Time Forgot 195
35. Final Flame for The Looted Plate 200

Shoulder It

Misci Papa kicked the old Vespa to life with a violent cough, a cloud of blue smoke billowing from the exhaust and hanging in the air like an old grudge. His hands, weathered and steady, gripped the handlebars while the boy — no older than eight or nine — stood next to him, heart pounding in eager anticipation. The old man's broad shoulders, carved from years of labour, seemed to carry the weight of the world. To the boy, this was the man who could make anything possible.

The helmet he jammed onto the boy's head stank of mildew and basement rust. It was far too big, sliding so the strap rubbed his neck in an annoying, scratchy way. He climbed on, gripping his grandfather's jacket, fingers finding nothing but the bony ridges of a man built strong. The Vespa shuddered beneath them as if it knew it was carrying more than it should.

Grandfather on his mother's side, Misci Papa was a saint — not the soft kind you see in paintings, but the kind who was always busy with something, never sitting still, always finding a way to be productive around the house. Roman Catholic through and through, he prayed before eating, prayed before working, prayed before sleeping. The kind of man who kissed Grandma's hand every time he saw her, not for show, but because that's what a gentleman did. His faith wasn't a decoration — it was built into him, like the calluses on his palms or the straightness of his back. And behind those steady eyes was a quiet wisdom that didn't need many words to be understood. In his jacket pocket, he always carried his rosary beads, their wood worn smooth from years of use.

He'd turn them slowly between his fingers while thinking, the beads clicking like a clock counting out his thoughts. When the prayers were done, they went back into his pocket — a talisman against whatever the world might throw at him.

And yet, alongside this devotion lived another obsession — one that seemed almost at odds with his saint-like discipline. He was obsessed with self-defence. Not the kind that involved shop-bought rifles or military surplus, but homemade contraptions cobbled together from whatever he could find. Old umbrellas, bits of pipe, springs from broken furniture — in his mind, these were the raw materials of survival.

His pride and joy was a homemade air gun he'd built in the shed. It was an ungainly thing, with the handle of an umbrella for a stock, a mismatched barrel that rattled if you shook it, and enough duct tape to make it look like a bad science experiment. He'd show it off with the seriousness of a man unveiling a prototype at a weapons expo, explaining how the air chamber worked, how the trigger was "improved" from last time, how the barrel was now slightly straighter.

In reality, the gun was weak. It couldn't hurt a pigeon unless the pigeon agreed to die out of politeness. The pellets barely made it out of the barrel, and more than once they dribbled out like the gun was ashamed of itself. But Grandpa never stopped tinkering. Each time he adjusted it, he claimed it was "much better now" and that "next time" it would be powerful enough to drop a rabbit at twenty paces. The gun was less about protection and more about readiness — never being caught helpless. Between the rosary in one pocket and a makeshift weapon in the other, Misci walked through life with God in one hand and his own stubborn ingenuity in the other. That day, they left Dunaújváros without a backward glance. Soviet concrete blocks shrank in the mirror, relics of a past nobody wanted but everyone carried. Asphalt gave way to dirt, dirt to something barely passable, the Vespa rattling over ruts deep enough to swallow ankles. Between them, ropes, sacks of sugar, and shopping bags of God knows what bounced in time with the engine. Misci's whistle cut the air — a signal to the neighbours: I'm coming. Pour the wine.

The shack by the Danube appeared, as it always did three times a week — his sanctuary from the city's stench. More patchwork than architecture, its walls were stitched together from whatever he'd managed to acquire, the roof groaning in winter and leaking when it pleased. Inside were tools, damson spirit, sacks of sugar, a few beds, a table — and anything else Misci decided was worth keeping.

His garden was pretty, purposeful. Rows of berry bushes fat with raspberries and strawberries. Apple and peach trees bowing under their own success. Ezerjó for wine, plums for pálinka. Everything here ate, drank, or burned — and nothing went to waste. Normally, this was the ritual. Getting away from the city, garden, wine, food, sleep, river. But today the ground had other plans.

Some trips were worse, when night rain turned the road into a pit. The Vespa made it a few metres before its wheels spun, coughing like an asthmatic in winter. Misci killed the engine, swung off, and yanked the boy down into the mud. His boots sank with a wet suck. They unloaded in silence. He handed the boy the lighter bags, but the moment the straps dug into his shoulders, he understood — he'd been given his share, and there would be no trading loads. Misci took the heavy stuff — rope, sugar, tools — as if it weighed nothing. The road ahead was brown glue.

"Get ready," he said. The first step nearly tore the boy's boot clean off. Each one after fought him, as if the road itself wanted him to fail. The mud clung and sucked, heavy as wet cement, dragging at his legs until every movement felt like lifting a sack of stones while sliding sideways. Misci moved like the corn they passed — tall, stubborn, unbent. The sunflowers turned their faces as they went by, as though they knew better than to ignore him.

Halfway through, the boy's legs burned, his chest rattled, the straps gnawed deep into his shoulders and palms. He wanted to quit. When Misci finally stopped for a breath, the boy tried to grab one of the heavier bags from him, desperate to prove he could carry more.

Misci just gave him a glance — the kind that didn't need words — and kept his load. But in that glance, he took the boy's measure. He admired the stubborn spark in him, couldn't quite believe how hard he was trying to show his strength. And yet, behind that grit were tiny, sinking steps, feet half-swallowed by mud, and the frame of someone far too young for this kind of road.

His voice came low, not angry, just absolute: "Pick it up, boy. Your load." And he did. Because quitting wasn't an option. Not here. Not with those eyes on him.

They trudged for over an hour before the shack's crooked silhouette appeared through the trees. Smaller now, hunched and waiting — but it meant they'd made it. By then, the boy was mud up to his knees. The Vespa was far behind, swallowed by the road.

At the time, the boy didn't get it. He was just a kid too young to understand work beyond what he could carry. Kitchens? Life? None of that made sense yet. He had two sisters, a house full of women, and the old man must have seen something in him — out of twelve cousins, there were plenty of boys like him, but the old man had already made his choice. This boy was his favorite, the one he wanted to shape.

It had never been about the sugar, or the rope, or the journey. It had been about a test — the kind he'd been planning quietly in his head. The kind you don't recognise until you're too far in to turn back.

That night, under scratchy army blankets in the drafty little cabin, skin stinging from cold and the effort, the boy learned the truth — at least part of it. Kitchens, life, whatever came later… none of it would be about talent alone. It would be about shouldering the load you've got, walking through the mud — no matter how deep — and not putting it down until the job's done.

A Rebel in the Gray

Hungary in the late '70s wasn't a postcard from paradise. It was a place where ambition went to die—crushed under the heavy boots of Communism. Everything was rationed: flour, meat, gasoline, hope. The streets were lined with bleak, Soviet-style concrete blocks, as if even the architecture had given up trying to inspire people.

But in one tiny apartment, chaos thrived — and at the center of it was Laszlo, a whirlwind rascal, too honest to cheat and too stubborn to sit still; the self-proclaimed terror of his teachers and the bane of his parents' existence.

Now, before we go any further, let's get the family gossip out of the way—the kind of juicy, small-town scandal that would make a soap opera writer jealous. According to whispered rumors—spread mostly by my grandmother, Rózsi néni from my father's side, who could spin a story better than most drunks at a wedding—my father might not have been a "pure Szűcs" at all. Supposedly, Grandma had a little fling with the local Gypsy king of Siófok, who, to spice things up, was also rumored to be Jewish. A Gypsy king and a Jew? In our village, that was like throwing gasoline on a bonfire. But more on that in the next chapter.

Laszlo's father wasn't exactly losing sleep over the rumors. He was the quiet, brooding type—more interested in books than genealogy. He'd sit in his favorite chair, puffing away on a cigarette, ash falling onto the pages of whatever thick, intellectual tome he was reading. Half-vanished behind a dense novel, eyes distant, lost somewhere between philosophy and paranoia.

He wasn't a bad father—not really. Just... mysterious. Shady, even. Lajos was technically a chemist, though you'd never guess it from the smell of him. He finished his schooling, sure—but instead of mixing compounds or saving the world from bad pharmaceuticals, he spent the next 37 years at Siófok's only petrol station where heating oil sold out mysteriously fast—especially to Turkish lorries..

Attached to the petrol station was a grim little café where the coffee was decent enough. Between fueling up Fiats and making backroom deals in motor oil, Lajos kept himself entertained behind the espresso machine—allegedly conducting a long-term 'nipple chemistry' study with whichever waitress was on shift. He and his mates spun tits like knobs on a busted radio, waiting for coffee like entitled maniacs who didn't give a damn. My mother knew. Everyone knew. It was practically part of the loyalty program.

He never hid it. None of them did. In his circle, cheating wasn't shameful—it was currency. Talking about it made you a man. Punching your wife in face every now and then? That made you a bigger one. These were supposed intellectuals.

Laszlo's bigger problem was dodging his father's belt whenever school got him in trouble. The beatings weren't malicious; they were more like a misguided attempt at parenting. His father wasn't the kind of man to talk about feelings or sit down for a heart-to-heart. No, he was a "discipline first, regret later" kind of guy. And he did regret it. After punishment, he'd retreat to his chair, light up another Marlboro, and bury his guilt somewhere between Kafka's bureaucratic nightmares, and that absurdly thick Winnetou novel by Karl May—1,200 pages of imaginary Native wisdom written by a German who'd never seen a horse. Laszlo's mother was the glue holding everything together. She was the kind of woman who could scrub a floor until it shone and whip up a hearty meal out of rationed ingredients—all while pretending not to notice the cigarette burns her husband left on the furniture. She didn't smoke, didn't yell, and somehow managed to keep the peace in a household that often felt like it was one raised voice away from implosion.

Laszlo, meanwhile, was a force of nature. The kind of kid who could charm the socks off you one minute and drive you to the brink of madness the next. He had no patience for rules or authority—especially not in school. Homework was a personal insult. Teachers were enemies. And Russian lessons? A cruel joke. He had no interest in learning the language of the people who kept his country under their boot.

Outside, the world was just as scrambled. The hippie movement had seeped into Hungary in a watered-down, state-approved version. Jimi Hendrix records were contraband, handed off like stolen arts in a country where guitars could get you watched. Laszlo's parents would sometimes host parties where the vodka flowed freely and the music played just a little too loud—brief escapes from the gray monotony of Communist life.

And then there was the political tension, always lurking in the background. People didn't talk about it openly—it wasn't the kind of thing you brought up at dinner unless you wanted your front door kicked in by Hungary's notorious State Protection Authority. But the frustration was palpable. Laszlo didn't fully understand it, he could only feel it in the way adults spoke, in their hesitation before answering certain questions. Three house searches before puberty. Not because anyone was rich—just his old man earning a little too fast, moving heating oil as diesel. The message was clear: don't get too clever. Don't get ahead.

After the fall, the Russian soldiers didn't invade—they wandered. Broke, abandoned, barely in uniform, they drifted through Hungarian towns. No orders. No money. Just state-issued junk and a burning obsession with wristwatches. They'd trade anything for one—blankets, boots, ammo, even bayonets—right there on the sidewalk. They'd press the watches to their ears, mesmerized by the ticking, like it was black magic. Most of them couldn't tell time—but for a moment, they could own it. Then they moved on. Always looking for another tick.

The Russians brought weapons. But the Poles invaded with plastic. They turned our food markets into flea markets, practically overnight. Every open space was swallowed by a forest of cheap goods—kitchen tools that broke on first use, inflatable toys, knockoff perfumes, plastic flowers, curtains, ashtrays shaped like pigs, wobbly clocks, wind-up Santas—even in July. It was relentless. Piles of it. Stuff no one asked for, but everyone bought.

The Polish sellers stood behind their stalls like conquerors, shouting prices in broken Hungarian, haggling like it was a blood sport. And we bought it. Because after years of grey shelves and state rations, even the illusion of choice felt like freedom. Looking back, it was early-stage consumerism with a Slavic accent—the same explosion of stuff we'd later get from the Chinese. Just louder. And slightly more religious.

For the boy in the corner with too many questions and not enough patience, Hungary felt like a cage—a small, polite, paprika-scented cage. The older he got, the more ridiculous it felt. Too many rules, too many fences, and too many people pretending everything was fine as long as the gulyás was hot and the radio played old dance hits from Yugoslavia.

When the family moved to Balatonszántód—a summer resort town that went from packed to post-apocalyptic by October—he realized the lake had two moods: sunburn and death. The silence after tourist season could drive a person to theology. Or theft. He didn't know where he wanted to go, only that it had to be a place with passports, palm trees, or small hum of life still going.

There was a kind of fever in him. Run, run, run—run, boy, run. Not from something. Not toward anything. Just away.

From boredom.

From plastic pigs.

From flea-market perfume and men who smelled like despair and smoke.

Beaten with Love (and a Backhand)

If my grandmother was the queen of lies, my grandfather was her court jester—a man so harmless and bumbling, he made Charlie Chaplin look like a symbol of efficiency. He was an alcoholic of the quiet type—no brawls, no shouting, just a slow drift into oblivion. He was a white wine enthusiast, the type who sipped his way into a quiet stupor, occasionally emerging to stumble into situations that were, frankly, too pathetic not to laugh at.

Football games were his escape. He loved them—well, as much as you can love something you're not technically allowed to watch. You see, Grandma would generously give him money for a ticket, but somehow, by the time he got to the gate, that money had magically transformed into a bottle of cheap wine. So instead of sitting in the stands like a normal person, he'd stand outside the stadium, peering through the concrete gate's gaps like a prisoner fantasizing about freedom. There he was, squinting and wobbling, trying to make out the game between the cracks while the rest of the crowd roared in unison behind him. If you ever wondered what the absolute bottom tier of human dignity looks like, there it was—dressed in mismatched socks and reeking of Sauvignon Blanc.

Meanwhile, Grandma ran her empire like a mob boss on a budget—small in stature, massive in mischief. If Hungary in the late '70s was a bleak, gray world, then my grandmother, was the Technicolor chaos cutting through it. A small woman with a big presence, she was known around town as the sweet lady with the red camping bicycle—a staple of the era, clunky yet somehow endearing, much like the woman herself. But let's not get too sentimental about her; she was also, without a doubt, the most accomplished liar I've ever met. My grandma didn't just lie—she lived lies. She lied with the grace of a ballerina and the confidence of a dictator. She lied even when she didn't need to, just for the sheer sport of it. If she was caught in a lie, she didn't backpedal or apologize. No, that would've been beneath her. Instead, she doubled down, piling on more lies like bricks in a wall until her original story was buried so deep, even she probably forgot what it was.

She worked as a cashier in the town's so-called "casino," more like a low-ceilinged graveyard of flashing junk slot machines. But even that's not quite fair, because back then it was part of one of Siófok's luxurious duty-free hotels — the kind that felt like portals to the West. These hotels lined Lake Balaton's shoreline like flashy outposts of another world, places where you could score your first pack of real bubble gum or a can of Coke — a miracle for kids raised on rationed basics.

The "casino" was actually the hotel's bowling alley, with a mini-golf course outside and the lake shimmering just beyond. It was loud, and tacky in the most glamorous way — a paradise of neon beer signs, bad disco, and the constant whiff of imported cigarettes. Outside, pastel-suited East Germans drifted along the Petőfi promenade, cocktails in hand, trying to look rich while their socks were still drying on the hotel balcony, convinced they were living the Riviera dream… just with more mosquito bites.

And right there, behind the cash register, stood Grandma—smiling sweetly, calculating quickly, and ruling her buzzing corner of capitalism like a queen in a kerchief. She worked late shifts, riding her red bike home under the dim streetlights. Everyone in town knew her and greeted her with smiles, but I'm pretty sure she had her own little side hustle going on. Rumor had it she skimmed tokens off the wealthy gamblers, keeping a secret stash that supplemented her income. It wasn't so much stealing as it was... creative accounting.

Her schemes weren't just limited to work; take the infamous chicken incident, for example. She somehow convinced my father to go halves with her on a batch of live chickens. "We'll raise them together," she said sweetly. "You'll get half the eggs, half the meat. It's a win-win!" What she conveniently failed to mention was that the chickens would all live in her backyard and she'd be the one in charge of feeding them.

Naturally, she demanded my father pitch in for the feed. Repeatedly. Week after week, she collected money for chicken food, claiming it was a huge expense. In hindsight, she probably fed them scraps—or nothing at all. Then one day, tragedy struck—well, convenient tragedy. She came to my father, all distraught, claiming that foxes had gotten into the coop and killed three chickens. And wouldn't you know it—all three of the missing chickens were his. What were the odds?

And then there was her relationship with my grandfather. If there was ever a man who could endure hardship with quiet dignity, it was him. He was the yin to her chaotic yang, a calm, passive soul who seemed content to weather her storms. But make no mistake—those storms were brutal. She'd berate him for any number of reasons, real or imagined, and when words weren't enough, she'd escalate to physical attacks. The chickens, the casino, the lies—all of it was just the tip of the iceberg. But her pièce de résistance, the true highlight of her domestic dominion, was the beatings she dished out to my grandfather. Now, don't get the wrong idea. These weren't violent, rage-fueled assaults. No, this was performance art. She would ask him into their bedroom, close the door softly—as if protecting the sanctity of their shared space—and then unleash a flurry of slaps that would echo through the thin walls like the drum solo of a bad garage band.

My sisters and I would sit in the kitchen, wide-eyed, trying to decipher the bizarre symphony. Slap, slap, slap! It was relentless. His back, in particular, seemed to be her favorite target—probably because it made the most satisfying noise. It was like she was auditioning for a percussion section, and Grandpa was her snare drum. What made it all the more surreal was the total lack of protest. No cries of pain, no shouts of defiance—just the rhythmic sound of hands meeting flesh.

And then, as if stepping out of a dream, she'd emerge from the room, smiling like a sweet old lady in a toothpaste commercial. "What are you kids up to?" she'd chirp, as if we hadn't just spent the last ten minutes listening to her turn Grandpa into a human bongo. My sisters and I would exchange looks, silently agreeing that whatever we were up to, it was far less insane than whatever was happening in that bedroom. Grandpa would shuffle out later, slightly disheveled but otherwise unbothered, like he'd just finished a yoga session rather than a beatdown. He never complained, never raised his voice. Maybe he was numb to it, or maybe he figured that enduring Grandma's wrath was easier than arguing with her. Or maybe he was too drunk to care.

Family rumors didn't help his case, either. According to whispers (mostly propagated by Grandma herself), Grandpa might not have even been my father's biological dad. The real father, she hinted, was a Gypsy king—a dark-skinned, tall, curly-haired charmer who also happened to be Jewish. Named Tichamér, and he fled Budapest carrying fourteen kilos of gold and a huge elephant-shaped statue carved from actual elephant bone. Said the gold would be enough to survive communism. Then he moved across the road.

Literally. Just across the highway from Lajos's petrol station, where he'd sip coffee in the café and flash his gold tooth at the man unknowingly raising his son.

To hear Grandma tell it, the Gypsy king had bestowed upon my father his black curly hair, dark(ish) skin, and a nose so large it could've been used as a sundial. "It's not my fault he looks like that," she'd say, waving her hand dismissively. "Blame the king." And yet, when you looked at me—blonde-haired, blue-eyed, a stark contrast to my father—it was clear that whatever genes the Gypsy king had contributed, they'd taken a hard pass on me.

Grandma, of course, reveled in these little stories. They were just another layer of her chaotic charm, another way to keep everyone guessing. Was she telling the truth? Was she lying for fun? Did she even know the difference anymore? It didn't matter. In her world, truth was flexible. Reality was optional. Grandma made life unpredictable, unapologetic, and weirdly delicious. And somehow, all of that made me who I am. She'd melt goose fat in her ancient iron pot, slide the liver in for a slow, silent ride through the oven, then leave it to cool overnight on the windowsill. By morning, it was entombed in golden fat like treasure. She'd dig it out, slice it paper-thin, and slap it onto toast slick with the same grease. No name. No fanfare.

The French gave it flair and a name you can't spell sober—Foie Gras. But Hungary had been at it for centuries. They rebranded it—we just served it with onions and bread.

And poor Grandpa? He just stood there, quietly sipping his wine, gazing through the gaps in the stadium gates, and probably wondering how the hell he ended up in this circus.

And so, Laszlo's legend grew. In his mind, he was a Gypsy prince, a culinary genius, and a political dissident—all rolled into one. The reality was slightly less glamorous: a boy with an overactive imagination, a talent for chaos, and a knack for turning even the dullest moments into epic sagas. But somewhere in that gray, crumbling world of Communism, a spark was lit. Laszlo didn't just dream of escaping—he dreamed of conquering, cooking, and creating a life so colorful it would make even Grandma's scarves look dull.

And so, with a wooden spoon in one hand and a stolen spice jar in the other, he prepared for his destiny.

The world, he decided, wasn't ready for him—but it would be.

The Basement of Blood

Patkó restaurant, the so-called crown jewel of Lake Balaton, was where I started my very first training— a place so chaotic it made lunatic asylums look well-managed.

Gyula Ohlmann ran the kitchen like a tyrant—a barrel-chested colossus with a booming voice that could shatter glass. A culinary warlord whose reputation preceded him, his apron was a battlefield of grease and blood, his face locked in a permanent scowl that made every second under his watch feel like combat training and a forest of back hair creeping out the collar of his shirt that made you rethink shaking hands.

Wild game was the star of the show: venison, wild boar, pheasant, rabbit, and whatever could be illegally shot in the woods after dark. I do mean illegally. After a full day sweating over stoves, Gyula and the owner Pálfi would dress head-to-toe in camo like retired mercenaries, disappear into the night—grimy, grinning, and probably on every forest ranger's watchlist. They'd load up an old grey Volvo station wagon and a muddy green Land Rover with rifles, ammo, and just enough pálinka to turn poor decisions into bold adventures.

Destination? The forests near Lulla or deep into Zemplény, where they'd hunt wild boar, deer, pheasant—anything with legs and a price tag. No rules. Just flashlights, silencers, and a hunger for profit. By sunrise, they'd roll back to the restaurant—mud-splattered, hollow-eyed, and hauling a crimson-drenched carload of fresh kills. The animals were butchered, portioned, plated, and sold by dinner. All for German tourists who toasted each overpriced venison steak like they were dining in some highland lodge, clueless that their "wild game" had been poached under moonlight and questionable legality.

"Faster! That dumpling won't cook itself, kisköcsög!" Gyula bellowed, slamming pans like war drums. Somehow, he always looked like he'd just wrestled a wild boar out back for fun.

But the real horror wasn't upstairs in the kitchen—it was in the basement, where the soul of this place (and its profits) lived. I descended into that crimson-stained dungeon alongside the owner's son, a pale, silent figure with the personality of a damp sponge, but with the focus of a sniper and the hands of a thief.

The basement hit like a waking nightmare. The smell struck first—old blood, wet fur, and something worse no one could name. Boars, deer, and rabbits dangled from hooks, swinging in the draft, their dead eyes glazed and indifferent. Blood dripped lazily onto cracked concrete, pooling in sticky puddles that never truly dried. A hose lay across our boots, coiled like a lazy python. Someone would spray it down now and then, but it made no difference—the stench had seeped into the bricks, our clothes, into everything. The walls bore streaks of dried gore, layer upon layer, a grotesque history painted in red.

My job was skinning, a skill I had to learn fast. I was sixteen. "Don't ruin the hide! That's money hanging there!" Gyula barked from the top of the stairs, his voice thundering down like a curse.

My hands trembled the first time I peeled a rabbit, the fur slipping off like a wet glove. But by the end of the first week, I could strip a deer faster than Gyula could hurl another insult.

Then there was Gyula's girlfriend—an untouchable queen among the carnage. She didn't belong in this chaos, and she knew it. Stunning, with flawless brown curls and a body sculpted by some cruel cosmic joke with the kind of presence that made you feel like a stray dog just for existing. Never lifted a finger, leaning against the wall with her arms crossed, her spotless sneakers miraculously avoiding the grime. I couldn't even look at her properly without my face burning; her very presence felt like a challenge I'd already lost.

This was Patkó: brutal, filthy, and absurd!

Upstairs, Eastern Germans—still clinging to their mullets and polyester dreams—cheered over overpriced venison steaks, trying desperately to impress their Western cousins. The Westerners sat smugly in Lacoste shirts tucked into high-waisted jeans, flashing Mercedes keys like they'd just bought East Germany and were still waiting for the receipt. They spoke loudly, slowly, as if volume and arrogance could substitute for vocabulary, then laughed like they invented forks.

They devoured goulash with the confidence of people who thought paprika was exotic. Their children poked at dumplings like they were alien life forms, and the waiters bowed and scraped as if Michelin stars might fall from the sky if they poured the mineral water just right. Meanwhile, downstairs, meat cleavers slammed through tendons. I was knee-deep in blood and boiling bones, wondering if this was what "success" in the restaurant world looked like. Up there was fine dining. Down here? It was trench warfare with aprons.

We were always starving. That deep, slow-burning kind of hunger that makes your ribs feel like they're gnawing back. We'd start before lunch service, crash through dinner, and by the time we dragged ourselves out the back door, it was pitch dark and the trash bins were the only things still steaming. Maybe we got one lunch break. Maybe. And it was always just enough food to tease your stomach, never enough to satisfy it. But we didn't complain. Not out loud.

Which was funny—because we worked at one of Lake Balaton's most reputable restaurants. Tourists lined up for goose liver, pheasant and venison. Imported wines were uncorked with flair, like liquid status symbols on every table. And down in the kitchen? The cooks were running on fumes, swallowing spit between courses, burning more calories in a shift than we could ever chew back in a day.

There was this kid in the kitchen—a cousin of the chef or something. My age, maybe younger. Skinny, fast, desperate. Just like the rest of us. And just like us, he was too scared to say he was hungry. Chef didn't tolerate weakness. You don't ask for more food in the middle of a war zone.

Until one day, the kid cracked. He stopped mid-shift, steam rising around him, eyes wild.

"We can't keep doing this," he said.
"We're hungry. Every day. It's not enough. We're working like animals and eating like rats!"

The room went dead silent. We all expected Chef to explode. Fire him on the spot. Maybe throw something. But he didn't. He walked to the pass, picked up a perfectly glazed confit goose leg, and handed it to the boy.

"Eat," he said.

We watched in stunned silence as the kid tore into it like a stray dog. Finished it.

Chef asked:
"Still hungry?"
"Yes."
He handed him a second goose leg.
Gone.
"Still hungry?"
"Yes."
A third goose leg. No one said a word. We just stared.

And Gyula—this monster of a man, usually all rage and elbows—looked at the floor like it had insulted him.

He didn't yell. Didn't kick the kid out. Didn't say anything at all. Just turned around and went back to the stove. And we did too. And that was it. We weren't starving because there wasn't food. We were starving because feeding us wasn't the point.

I thought I'd seen the worst. Midnight-poached venison, Gyula screaming in my face like a drunk Viking. But then I got sent to Germany. And found out what hell really smells like. My father arranged it. Said it would "build character." A summer job at a restaurant in Germany, by the postcard waters of Lake Chiemsee. He meant well. He didn't know they'd throw me straight into hell. I was still a child, fresh out of chef school. What he didn't know was that I'd start every morning elbow-deep in a bathroom marinated in last night's beer parade.

I had to clean the men's toilet.
At six a.m.
Every day!

After a full night of Bavarian piss had been left to ripen like radioactive sauerkraut. Warm air, stale beer, bratwurst acids, and twelve hours of unchecked bladder mayhem. It smelled like God had left the building and the devil ran the plumbing. My mop disintegrated on day two. After that, I was allowed in the kitchen—not to cook, but to exist. Chop this. Stir that. Shut up. Don't ask. Touch the wurst, lose a finger.

The owner barked in a language I didn't understand, and I refused to learn. German sounded like someone arguing with gravel in their mouth. Ugly words for an ugly job. I learned nothing. Except that I'd never learn German. Not for this. Not for anyone. I left after a few weeks.

Back in Hungary, time slid past. I floated through summers at Lake Balaton, working small jobs, chasing girls, drinking, and convincing myself I was growing up. I wasn't. And just when I thought the years would keep melting like that forever—one day, they didn't. I wasn't ready. I got married.

Blood-Red Gold

You know that sad red powder you bought in a plastic shaker for £1.99 at the supermarket? Do yourself a favor — throw it straight in the bin. That's not paprika. That's the cremated remains of a bell pepper that died of boredom.

Real paprika stains your fingers, your clothes, and possibly your soul. It's not a seasoning — it's a national fuel source. In Hungary, it's the first spice a baby smells and the last thing sprinkled on a dying man's soup. We don't just use it — we marinate in it, breathe it, and, on a bad day, probably sweat it.

By the end of summer, my mother's porch was drowning in peppers. Strings of them dangled from the beams like exotic trophies — swaying in the breeze, snapping and crunching when the wind blew too hard. Morbid. Gorgeous.

She'd sort them like a general preparing for battle — some kept whole for later missions, others sentenced to the grinder to become devil's dust, hoarded in old coffee jars like contraband. The seeds? Those were the real black-market goods. Duller in color, twice as cruel — the pepper world's equivalent of a shiv.

Sometimes she'd skip the chopping entirely, grab a dried one whole, and throw it straight into the pot without ceremony. Just violence. Boom. You knew dinner was going to be biblical when the air filled with that sweet, burning perfume — the smell of a warm, edible explosion.

In Hungary, paprika isn't "a spice." It's a form of hard currency. It's foreplay. It's a national blood type. And the wrong kind? It'll turn your pörkölt the color of wet mud and taste like boiled cardboard.

That Édesnemes is for softies, and Erős is for the maniacs. There are eight types, officially. But really, there are only two kinds: the one your mother approves of, and the one that gets you disowned. We don't measure it by teaspoons. We measure it by how red the oil turns, how deep the aroma stings your eyes. If you cough when it hits the pan, you're doing it right.

Yeah, yeah, vitamin C, Nobel prize, some guy named Szent-Györgyi isolated it from paprika — big deal. We never cared about the science. We just knew it kept us alive in winter. It was our pharmacy and our perfume. You want antioxidants? Iron? Vitamin E from the seeds? Sure. But we didn't grind seeds for health. We did it because they made the stew taste like hell and smoke had a baby. The kind of flavor that made your neighbour's eyebrows raise and your grandfather mutter, "Finally, someone cooked like a man."

The best paprika comes from Kalocsa or Szeged. These aren't towns — they're spice mafias. Entire families living off red powder. If you're born there, it's in your lungs. You come out of the womb coughing capsanthin. These towns don't mess around. EU PDO status. Color index measurements. Seed-to-grind laws. It's like cocaine but legal and edible. You can't just throw the name "Szegedi" on a packet. They'll come for you. Real paprika smells like sweet fire. You open the bag and suddenly you're in your grandmother's kitchen with a wooden spoon about to be smacked across your hand.

It's oily, not dry. It stains. It's packed in foil, not a plastic jar next to the oregano. If you can see the spice through the packaging, don't buy it. It's already dead.

And it has a use-by date shorter than your average TikTok scandal. Six months after opening and it turns into red sand. We go through ours in six weeks. Or six days if someone's in a mood and making halászlé.

Dirty Tricks & Old Wives' Wisdom

Want to know how Hungarians cheat? We toast the paprika in goose fat. Just a second. Not too long or it'll go bitter. But do it right and the entire block will smell like you're hiding a culinary crime scene.

Or we steep whole dried pods in oil for weeks — blood-red paprika oil, good enough to baptize your children in.

Some of us even add a pinch of sugar — not to sweeten it, but to deepen the color, trick the tongue, play a little flavor mind game. Paprika is a weapon. A seduction. A mask.

You Can Leave Hungary, But…

Every Hungarian abroad has a little jar of home hidden in the cupboard. Labeled with marker, smuggled in luggage, or mailed by a mother with a warning: "Do not buy foreign paprika."

We cook in exile, but with paprika, it's like we never left. It's our last tie to the soil. The smell of a homeland we may curse, escape, or forget — until dinner.

And even if we cook Michelin food now, private cheffing for politicians or prepping duck for billionaires on a yacht, we still keep a stash of paprika in the bag. Because one day, someone will ask for "a proper stew." And we'll give them Hungary in a spoon.

The Great Goulash Confusion

Outside Hungary, the word "goulash" has been hijacked to mean pörkölt, especially when it's a paprika-rich stew. So when foreigners say "Hungarian Goulash," they almost always mean pörkölt, the thick, meaty stew that sticks to your ribs and comes steaming from a pot cooked down with onions, lard, and paprika. But that's not gulyás. Not really.

Real gulyás is a soup. A herdsman's soup. Born on the sweeping plains of the Alföld, where cowboys called gulyás simmered their day's catch over open fires in cast-iron cauldrons. It was simple and satisfying — a bowlful of beef, root vegetables, and stock spiked with the newly beloved spice of the 18th century: paprika.

The paprika came later, after Turkish influence and a few curious farmers discovered it wasn't just some ornamental pepper. Once Hungarians got their hands on it properly, it changed everything.

But pörkölt — that thicker, richer cousin — didn't rise until the 19th century. That wasn't a cowboy meal. That was otthon, at home, in the kitchen. Urban, slow-cooked, lovingly stirred. The kind of dish that gets better overnight. Beef or pork, onions caramelized down in lard, paprika tossed in just after the onions to bloom in the fat — not too early, or it'll go bitter — then meat, water, lid, patience. I've had tourists swear they've had "authentic goulash" and describe something that's nowhere close to gulyás. "It was like a chili with elbow macaroni in it!" No, my friend. That was a Midwestern casserole that got lost in translation.

My Version of Gulyás — A Cowboy's Soup, Refined

The traditionalists might raise an eyebrow, but I like my gulyás with a few precise tweaks. It's still true to its roots — beef shank or chuck, onions, carrots, potatoes, a hint of garlic, paprika, and stock — but here's where I diverge:

Whole cumin seeds. They crackle in the oil early on, just after the onions. That warm, earthy aroma deepens the broth. It's not standard in every recipe, but it should be. The cumin gives the soup a deeper, slightly smoky backbone.

Precision matters. I dice the carrots and potatoes just small enough so that each spoonful delivers the full experience — a cube of beef, a piece of carrot, a chunk of potato, all suspended in that fiery red broth, perfectly balanced on the spoon.

It's peasant food made with surgeon's precision. And when done right, every bite is complete — meat, veg, broth, soul.

But for now, remember: If it's thick like stew, it's not gulyás. If it fits in a spoon and warms your chest from the inside out — it probably came from a Hungarian cowboy.

Pharaohs Don't Do Room Service

1996, as a wedding gift, someone thought it would be romantic to send us to Egypt. The cradle of civilization, they said. A river cruise on the Nile. Luxor. Aswan. The Giza pyramids. The gods would smile on our marriage.

They probably did. Or maybe they laughed.

It started with lamb at McDonald's. Cairo's golden arches served burgers made from something that once bleated. Beef was a myth—replaced by something that died confused and tasted like it had been aged in a sunbaked backpack. Outside, goats were being skinned on sidewalks. The air was thick with diesel, dust, and a smell I couldn't place—until I saw it. A butcher's shop with half a goat hanging by its ankles, jerking gently in the sun like it was trying to escape. Covered in flies. Glowing with bacteria. Customers strolled by like it was a flower shop, like half a goat doing a slow death-dance was just background decoration.

Our first night was in a hotel that smelled of death. Not metaphorical death—real, putrefying, something-is-definitely-dead death. Something was rotting under the stairs. A body? A dog? A cursed wheel of cheese? No one knew. The staff avoided the staircase. It may as well have had teeth.

I lay down on the bed in our cabin, we are on the river now. My new wife stepped into the bathroom.

My eyes closed. And that's when the dream began.

The Nile ran smooth beneath the boat, a black ribbon of mystery sliding through the desert. The ship gleamed, polished to distraction. And on deck? Dozens of tourists vomiting into napkins. Day one of the cruise, and we were all poisoned by the buffet. The lentils, the salad, the "fish"—all-inclusive misery. I clutched my market souvenir: a tiny crocodile. Dead. Rotting. Already stinking up our cabin. By morning, the crew blamed the smell on the plumbing. I said nothing.

Then came the temples.

KomOmbo: I wandered off, lured by a whispering cat. Down an alley that didn't exist on the map, I found a carved tablet—an alien holding a golden orb, etched in perfect symmetry. Beneath it: ancient Egyptian script that spelled my name. Laszlo. I touched it. My hands glowed. A man in robes handed me a coin. No explanation. Then vanished.

Edfu: The Temple of Horus hummed. Literally. A deep, low vibration that rattled my teeth. A guide gave no reason—just told me not to look up. Naturally, I did. The ceiling shifted. Stars realigned. The Eye of Ra blinked.

At Luxor, she disappeared. Gone. Vanished mid-tour, between hieroglyphs and a spice stall that reeked of sweat and cinnamon. I searched everywhere. Panic clawed through my chest. No guide, no passport, no plan. Just heat and sand and a growing suspicion that something wrong was unfolding. I found her two days later, at the camel market in Birqash. Camels. Market sounds. Shouting, spitting, ropes whipping through air. I bent over, trying not to vomit up what little water I'd hallucinated drinking. She wore flowing Egyptian robes, gold bangles, and hennaed hands. Her face was painted. Her eyes glazed. She was holding a camel by the reins in one hand and haggling in Arabic like she'd been doing it for decades. She didn't recognize me. Not even a blink.

"Madam," I said, "you're my wife."
She laughed.
"I've never seen you before in my life, white man."
I reached for her. The camel bit me.

When I came to, I was in the passenger seat of an old Land Cruiser, engine snarling, tires sliding across endless dunes. I was wearing robes. Not hotel-issued towels—real desert robes, burnished ochre, flapping like wings in the wind. A woven scarf was wrapped around my head. A curved dagger bounced against my hip. I looked like a man who knew the stars by name.

The heat was thick. Breathing felt like sucking air through a boiled blanket. The wind had that slap-in-the-face quality that makes you want to punch a stranger just for existing.

We passed the edge of the city, then the edge of sense. A crumbling airstrip with no planes. A barbed wire fence that fenced nothing. And a goat chewing on a tire, slow and deliberate, like it was settling an old score.

A boy selling dates had shouted something at me earlier:
"المختار المجنون إنت!"
("You are the chosen madman!")
At least I think that's what he said.
Or maybe he was just insulting my sandals.

My driver wore mirrored sunglasses and never moved a muscle.
He said only one thing:
"Tutankhamun's tomb is the decoy."

We drove for hours. Sandstorm rising. Sand lashing the windshield like razor blades. The horizon dissolved into a boiling wall of dust. The Land Cruiser kept moving, steady as a heartbeat carved from steel. The radio played nothing but static—then, music. Deep, rhythmic tones. Not drums. Older than drums. Like the earth was remembering a song no one taught it.

Then the driver pulled over. In the middle of nowhere. He stepped out, dropped to his knees, and began to pray. Facing the wind. Facing something. I stood beside him. Robes flapping. Head bowed. Dust in my teeth. Scarf around my face. Looking like I belonged to the land. Or was being eaten by it. Somewhere behind us, the dunes shifted like breathing lungs.

No words.
Just the prayer.
The storm.
The music of a world older than memory.

Then he stood. Brushed off his knees. Got back in.
And we drove on.

In the distance, a structure.
Not a pyramid.
Something lower. Wider. Glowing faintly.

I felt gold beneath the sand.
Mechanisms older than history.
This was no tomb.
This was an engine.
A power station.
Built not by pharaohs—but visitors.
Builders with long fingers and eyes like glass.

The cruiser stopped.
The driver handed me a key.
"You've been chosen," he said.
Then he melted into light.

I stepped forward.
The sand shifted.
The world tilted.
And I woke up.

Sweating in our tiny cabin, the ship lurching. My wife groaned beside me, finally recovering from the buffet massacre. The crocodile was gone. The window showed nothing but endless water—and on the far bank, a group of black kids hurling giant rocks into the river. Not fishing.

No aliens. No gold. No camels. But the smell of the hotel?

Still in my nose. And yet...
my fingers still glowed.
Just a little.

The Black Bridge Inn

Grandma wasn't just a haggler—she was a predator. At the street market, she hunted chickens with the focus of a sniper and the charm of a car crash.

"Józsi, don't insult me with these feathers. Did you pluck it in the dark?" she'd say, holding up a limp bird like it personally offended her.

She was an artist—smiling while she hunted, pouring honey in your ears while she picked your stall clean.

"Józsikám, you always save the best for me, don't you?" she'd purr, patting the vendor's arm while locking eyes with the fattest chicken on the table. He'd smile nervously, unsure whether he was being charmed, tricked, or both. The answer was always both.

She moved from stall to stall like a general surveying her troops—narrow-eyed, purse tucked under her arm like ammunition, looking for the one chicken that looked perfect and hadn't been touched by grubby buyer hands.

And me? I wanted to disappear. I was five, maybe six, trailing behind her like a tiny hostage. Every second was agony. It was like watching a Turkish bazaar performance.

She'd linger just long enough to wear them down, never arriving up at peak hour. No—she waited. She lingered like perfume in the air. When the sun was high, when the vendors were tired, sweaty, hungry—that's when she struck. Always with a compliment, always with a smile.

Now? I'd laugh. Now, I'd pay money to watch her work. Her legendary chicken broth? Soul-healing. Otherworldly. Worth every casualty.

But for all her fire and folklore, Grandma had a colder side too. One that didn't ask, didn't explain, and didn't apologize.

Like the time my father brought home two white Kuvasz puppies—massive, bear-like Hungarian dogs with paws too big for their bodies and hearts even bigger.

We'd begged for pets. Begged. And when we finally got them, it felt like Christmas and a royal coronation rolled into one. But we lived in a cramped little apartment, no room for dogs to roam. So we did the only thing that made sense—we sent them to Grandma's place temporarily. Just a few weeks in her backyard. Just until they settled in.

And then... they were gone. No warning. No explanation. She gave them away. Just like that.

We were devastated. Me, my siblings, my father—we cried. He was furious, heartbroken, blindsided. She never said why. Never admitted it. Never even seemed to notice the fallout.

That was Grandma. One moment she's ladling broth that could raise the dead. The next, she's erasing something you love—and moving on like nothing happened. And yet, for all her schemes and contradictions, she left fingerprints on my soul. Thirty years later, I'd haggle over "smart chickens" at the Santa Monica Farmers Market—channeling her flair, her instinct, her charm. I'd brew tea the way she did, mixing five or six loose-leaf varieties into one strange, magical blend no one could name but everyone loved. Even the lies, the silent decisions, the vanished dogs—they taught me something too: that love isn't always gentle, but it can still leave a mark.

My formal culinary training began under Ohlmann Gyula, but it was our family's Black Bridge Inn that truly ignited my passion. The Inn, affectionately called Hordó by locals. It wasn't just a restaurant; it was an immersive experience. Candlelit garden, open-flame grills, and our family—half hospitality experts, half circus troupe.

My mother ran the bar out of a literal barrel, my sisters and cousins charmed guests as waitresses, and my father, well... he perfected the art of doing absolutely nothing. Dad held court at the cash register, occasionally strolling through the dining room like a king inspecting his serfs. His real kingdom, however, was upstairs, where he read books and chain-smoked like an intellectual recluse. When the chaos below reached fever pitch, he'd descend dramatically, nodding approvingly, then vanish back to his fortress.

It was late—close to closing—and like clockwork, the troublemakers arrived. Not the decent local folk who came for just a drink, but the rowdy breed. The kind of customers who drank too much, shouted too loud, and always seemed to think they were on the verge of starting a revolution, or a fistfight. These were tourists, or sailors maybe. Already six pálinkas too deep, swaying at the heavy wooden tables like they were riding out a storm. This time, one of them made a comment about my sister's uniform skirt. Now, to be fair, the skirts were short—part of the rustic charm, apparently—but the guy's tone was all wrong. Her boyfriend Gyula heard it, and things turned fast. Words were exchanged. Voices raised. You know where this goes.

We also asked them to leave. They didn't. Arguments flared. Then the kitchen emptied. My sister Judit, Gyula, the cooks—Csaba, the strongest among us—plus a couple more boys, flexible cooks, a Roma dishwasher whose name I don't remember. My mother. Even my father came down from upstairs like Zeus from Mount Olympus.

The restaurant turned harbor. Benches flipped. Bottles rolled across gravel.

One of the sailors took a wild swing at Gyula—missed. I grabbed him by the collar, slammed him against the fence so hard it rattled like a loose sail in wind. Another lunged at me. I ducked, caught him with a knee to the gut, and he folded like laundry.

Csaba went straight into the thick of it. No yelling, just fists. Clean, brutal punches—one-two combos that looked practiced. A sailor tried to grab him from behind. Big mistake. Csaba swung around and dropped him with an elbow to the cheek that cracked loud enough to silence a dog.

And then—my mother.

She didn't walk. She stormed. Spotted a loose plank from the old garden gate lying in the corner. She picked it up—two-handed, like a sword. And she went to town on one of the guys. Whack! Whack! A flurry of righteous fury, wielded by a woman who once raised three kids on war rations and rage.

The next morning, I stepped outside, eyes half-shut, still tasting the adrenaline of the night before. And there it was—the stick. Lying in the gravel like Excalibur, waiting for the next chosen one. I picked it up. It was heavier than I remembered. And then I saw them: long, rusty nails jutting out from the side. Bent and wicked, like some medieval torture weapon. My mother beat a grown man with a spiked club. And I haven't stopped laughing since. Because nothing says family-run restaurant like a goose confit special followed by a full-contact brawl in the garden.

Meanwhile, I was the chef, clad in a tall hat that screamed "authority." Guests marveled as I wielded my tongs like a blacksmith forging thunder, sending flames shooting into the night sky. Locals joked that the scent of my grilling was more effective than church bells at drawing crowds.

And the crowds were characters—pure P. Howard madness. Feri, built like a cellar door, was perpetually drunk and ready to arm-wrestle anything that moved. The Brylcreem boys preened and struck out with waitresses. Karcsi bácsi, the village riesling-sipping gardener, growled insults at anyone who got too close.

Every night was a live comedy show starring unruly locals, drunken escapades, and waitresses dodging overly enthusiastic suitors. Live music. Endless flames on the grill. And once—just once—we had a professional opera singer join us. Not as a guest. As a temp table cleaner.

He'd wipe a table, clear a plate—and then suddenly launch into a full-throated aria that made wine glasses tremble. The whole restaurant would freeze. Conversations stopped. Cigarettes hovered in midair.

His voice was massive. Sharp, emotional, outrageous. Customers went wild. Some clapped. Some cried. One guy dropped his fork. He stayed for three days, then vanished just as suddenly as he appeared—like a baritone spirit sent to bless the chaos.

By the end of the evening, we'd drag ourselves to another bar, ready to relive the madness over beers until dawn. We weren't just feeding people—we were entertaining them. Leaving diners laughing and hooked. But here's the truth—

my whole family and every single staff member worked themselves into the ground, day after day, for four blistering months. My cousin Zsuzsa was there, always in motion, her smile lighting up the dining room. Years later, she died from an overdose. Her boyfriend was blamed—and he deserved every bit of it.

Shotomajor, my other cousin—that was his nickname—took on the thankless tasks without complaint, the kind of guy who kept the whole machine running while no one was watching. My sisters, cousins, the cooks, the dishwashers, my mother—even my father, drifting down from upstairs like royalty during peak hours—they all poured themselves into that place.

The ribs were the main culprits, slathered in our house bbq sauce—sweet and sharp and borderline addictive. The sauce didn't come from Hungary. It came from California—via my brother-in-law, John Maydeck, a man who treated BBQ like religion and ribs like scripture. We didn't use plates. We used wooden boats—massive, hand-carved platters made by the local gypsies. Each one a little crooked, no two were the same. Some looked like rafts, others like weapons. But once we loaded them with meat and carried them out—smoking, sizzling, heavy as hell—no one cared.

People came for the show as much as the food. The hiss of the grill. The flames licking the edges. The smell that made tourists pull over and ask, "What is that?"

It wasn't glamorous. It wasn't romantic. But it was relentless.

Summers were punishing—we served over 11,000 main courses in just four months. Then came winter. The restaurant closed. We lived off the summer takings, which vanished faster than a bowl of Grandma's chicken broth on a cold night.

After one especially brutal season in 1993, I escaped to California to visit my sister. It was a much-needed break—but it planted a seed. By 1998, I'd made the decision to stay. I left the Black Bridge Inn behind.

I didn't want it to, but without me, the place faltered. The magic leaked out. The family energy dimmed. Something essential went missing—some rhythm we'd conjured every night like a spell.

My parents' strained relationship unraveled. Dad rented it out to new management.

But the magic was gone. The fire went out. And nobody ever cooked ribs like that again. Guests missed the chaos, the characters, the fiery spectacle at the grill.

By the second summer, the doors closed for good.

Kitchen Hopper, California Dreamin'

As a teenager, I developed a peculiar habit I called kitchen-hopping. It wasn't a career path—it was more like culinary trespassing. I'd slip into the kitchens of local restaurants, charm the staff just enough to get hired for a few days. Why stay in one place when you can learn from them all?

The truth is, I was more thief than chef back then—not of money, but of knowledge. One kitchen smelled like burnt butter and ambition. Another hissed with steam and secrets. Everything was interesting. Head chefs ruled like tyrants, sous chefs translated the madness and every dishwasher a quiet philosopher with wet shoes knew when the next pan was going to fly before anyone else did.

I'd love to say I was a culinary prodigy destined for greatness, but no—I was more like a mosquito in a toque. I'd breeze through for a couple weeks, stir things up, pocket the good stuff, and vanish before anyone figured out what I was really after.

By my twenties, Hungary felt suffocating. The year was 1998—Communism's remnants were fading, the dot-com bubble was swelling, and Bill Clinton was in the news for things other than his saxophone skills. I needed an escape hatch. Enter my sister, phoning from California, where she lived with her husband, John Maydeck. John was so quintessentially American he could've been grilling burgers while waving a flag. But his true passion wasn't just my sister—it was his family's BBQ sauce. Thick, smoky, tangy—it was bottled patriotism. The recipe? It's in here. You'll find it later. Trust me—worth the wait.

John took me under his wing. He combined my kitchen-hopper charm with his relentless persistence, and together, we set our sights on The Plumed Horse, a restaurant with a reputation sharper than its steak knives. When Patrick Farjas, the head chef, heard John's pitch, he simply said, "Yes."

Welcome to the Culinary Arena: picture this. You step into a kitchen that feels like a steam-powered locomotive barreling at full speed. Flames dance in pans, knives flash under fluorescent lights, and the air vibrates with a chaotic symphony of clattering pots, shouted orders, and French profanity.

This is The Plumed Horse: a temple of gastronomy where perfection is the goal, chaos is the norm, and the absurd is always on the menu. Nestled in the trees of Saratoga, The Plumed Horse felt less like a restaurant and more like a secret. To your left, Marc the pastry chef pipes chocolate into molds shaped like jazz instruments while humming Coltrane. He sways as though conducting an invisible orchestra, exuding the air of someone who believes he's descended from French royalty—or at least Napoleon.

Marc's desserts were edible jazz solos: intricate, unpredictable, occasionally baffling. His signature dish? A To'ak chocolate pentagram filled with caramel mousse, garnished with edible gold, served on plates fit for the Louvre. "Laszlo," Marc once declared, hand on my shoulder like a knighting ceremony, "desserts are not food. They are emotions."

At the back, José, Eduardo, Miguel, and Juanito weren't just the backbone of the kitchen—they were its beating heart, albeit one with bad teeth and questionable fashion choices. None of them spoke English, at least not enough to string together a coherent sentence, but they didn't need to. They spoke the universal languages of hard work and sarcasm. Long hours had left their faces weathered, and hygiene wasn't exactly a priority. One of them—the self-appointed boss—dressed like a Chairman of the underworld board, slick shirt unbuttoned halfway down, chest hair glistening with the sweat of arrogance. He strutted around as if he were running the place, looking down on the others with the smug disdain of a telenovela villain.

Then there was The Double Agent, who worked at another restaurant just down the street. Between shifts, he brought us key intel: gossip about rival chefs, how busy they were, and once, the exact time their lobster shipment arrived. He guarded his information like state secrets, whispering in hushed tones, "Los de allá están cerrando temprano hoy," before vanishing into the heat and noise.

And let's not forget the wine guy. He stood at his station like he was waiting for an opera cue, sneaking gulps of wine with all the finesse of a raccoon in a trash can. He thought he was invisible, but Patrick's hawk-like eyes saw everything. That bottle cost him a month's wages.

Whenever Patrick wasn't around, the back kitchen transformed into a mariachi festival. Someone would crank up Mexican music—blaring corridos or rancheras loud enough to rattle the pans. "¡Ándale, cabrones!" they'd yell, laughing as the music drowned out the hum of the exhaust fans. As soon as Patrick's footsteps echoed down the hall, the volume would drop faster than soufflés in a thunderstorm.

Out front was Josh, one if the many waiters with the charm of a used car salesman and the hustle of a Wall Street broker. He could sell ice to Eskimos—or convince rich diners their $300 bottle of wine tasted like "a walk through a Tuscan vineyard." Somehow, this shady charmer became part-owner of The Plumed Horse and even helped earn it a Michelin star. "Josh?" Marc said, incredulous. "The guy who thought soufflé was cheese?"

Saratoga was home to wealthy eccentrics, and their requests were pure comedy. One man wanted his steak "medium-rare but fully cooked." Another insisted on vegan lobster soufflé. Patrick nearly fainted. A vineyard owner once tipped us with bottles of his own awful wine. Marc repurposed it to clean pastry molds. And let's not forget the Yelp "critics," nibbling Foie Gras like detectives and writing reviews as if we'd served them instant ramen.

Running the show was Patrick Farjas, a French chef with the soul of an artist, the patience of a saint. Born in Lyon, the culinary capital of the world, Patrick carried the weight of that legacy effortlessly. He wasn't just a chef; he was a maestro of ingredients.

Truffles were his muse. He stored truffles in jars, shaved thin and bathed in cognac. The scent alone could make you believe in heaven. Whether imported from France or foraged in Oregon, he treated them with huge respect. His obsession with mushrooms was almost spiritual. Porcini, chanterelle, matsutake, morels, white and black truffles—these weren't just ingredients; they were his gospel. Patrick would grab a blistering hot iron pan and drop in thick slices of duck liver—no oil, no nonsense. A hard sear in seconds, flip, out, set a side to rest. Heat still raging. He'd toss in a handful of sugar, let it melt and darken just enough, then throw in fresh black currants. The berries hit the duck fat and popped like gunfire. All of this—thirty, forty seconds tops. Then came the verjus—had to be verjus, nothing else gave it that sharp, clean snap. Now you had berries blistered in duck fat, swimming in a sweet-sour, bubbling, black-violet jus. He'd slide the liver back in, just to warm, just until the waiter showed up with the plate. Magic. Ruthless, fast, perfect.

Todd was tall and wiry, like a walking mushroom himself, with the alert posture of someone who'd just crawled out of the underbrush clutching chanterelles and wild sorrel like treasure. He'd glide into the kitchen like a cryptid, his wooden crate of earthy treasures cradled like a newborn. Patrick dropped everything — mid-sentence, mid-sauce, didn't matter — and rushed to the box like a man possessed.

He examined each mushroom with the care of a diamond dealer. If the batch was subpar, he'd wave Todd off with a sharp, "Non! Mushrooms deserve respect. Tu sens ça? C'est la forêt qui parle." (Smell that? That's the forest speaking.) But when the good stuff arrived, the kitchen came to a standstill. The earthy aroma filled the walk-in like nature's own cologne.

Todd and I became friends. He wasn't just a forager — he was a true gourmand, aging his own balsamic, running kingofmushrooms.com, and treating wild ingredients like sacred artifacts. The man lived for the forest. And thanks to him, so did our menu.

Patrick's search for baby vegetables was constant—tiny carrots, turnips, radishes, miniature romanesco, zucchini and baby cauliflower—so delicate they deserved birth certificates. His rack of lamb was a masterpiece: olive oil, raw onion, black pepper, seared to perfection—eight minutes on one side, five on the other—and voilà—pink, tender, flawless! Lobster was another of his symphonies, a creamy, truffle-laden marvel. Whether it was filet mignon, Florida Stone Crab Claws, bison, Alaskan Black Cod, or Chilean halibut, Patrick mastered every dish with precision and purpose, each ingredient playing a vital role.

As the quiet Hungarian with no English and everything to prove. Half the time, I didn't even know what I was looking at. So I wrote it all down, names, notes, recipes. Over time, I became the one he counted on.

With Patrick, I learned more than cooking. I learned how to finish things properly—and how to stay calm when a storm hit the line. After service, we'd square off on Yahoo! Chess. Patrick didn't teach with words — he taught by making you watch, sweat, and screw it up until you got it right.

His bacon? Slabs of pork belly, sugar, salt, star anise, black pepper, garlic paste, chili flakes — hung to dry until it smelled like God was curing meat in the back room.

His confit goose leg? Heavy salt on the skin, light sugar on the meat, garlic crushed, bay leaves jammed in like afterthoughts. Slow-cooked in duck fat until the bones poked out like white flags.

His abalone? Pound it thin, flour, egg, butter, lemon, one splash of cream.

No recipes taped to the wall. No laminated cheat sheets, just instincts.

Watching Patrick work—steady hands, no waste, no ego—was like watching another species. Maybe that's what scared me most: that beneath the wreckage and roar of kitchens like Patkó, there was another way.

Angel from Hungary

If my life were a soap opera, this chapter would've been the one where the writers ran wild—heartbreak, online romance, and an „Italian" girlfriend who belonged in a traveling sideshow rather than a studio apartment.

Let's start with my first wife, Krisztina—the same one who joined me on that surreal honeymoon in Egypt, haggling for camels and disappearing in Luxor like a reincarnated priestess. That was before everything started to fall apart. Our marriage lasted just two years. We were young and not quite built to last. Two years felt like a lifetime—in the best and hardest ways.

Things really began to unravel after we arrived in the U.S. Her tourist visa raised a few red flags at customs. She showed up with a 12-month return ticket, even though she was only allowed to stay for six. The customs officers may as well have slapped a neon sign on her forehead that read Potential Overstayer. She swore it was a simple mistake. I wanted to believe her.

But between the raised eyebrows at the airport and the growing tension between us, it was clear we weren't exactly destined for a fairy-tale ending. Meanwhile, I was juggling heartbreak and filet mignon at work, leaning on Patrick, my French culinary sensei, to pull me through. His advice was always straightforward: "Stop crying over women, focus on your cooking, and pour yourself a glass of wine—but not too much, Laszlo, or you'll ruin the sauce."

And then came Simone.

She claimed to be Italian, but honestly, she wasn't fooling anyone. She said "mamma mia!" more than a gondolier in peak season, and the closest she ever got to being Italian was twisting open a jar of marinara. Just to round things out, she wasn't even pretty. Not that it mattered, since she made up for her lack of beauty with an endless supply of bad attitude.

Her skin was a wonder of biology—pale white one moment, bright red the next, especially if something slapped it, like a hand or a gust of wind. She wasn't just high-maintenance; she was a walking, talking beauty regime.

Every morning, our tiny studio transformed into a full-scale cosmetic laboratory. There was a lotion for her arms, a spray for her legs, and some sort of magical potion for her toes—each with a distinct and overwhelming scent that fought for dominance in the air. Then came the nails. All twenty of them.

Every!   Single!   Morning!

She clipped, filed, and buffed like her life depended on it, while I lay in bed, clinging to the last shreds of sleep before she sprayed the room with citrus mist.

By 7:30, I was fuming. By 8:00, I was roaring out the door on my Yamaha, leaving behind nothing but tire marks and resentment. I can't be sure, but I think my motorcycle revved louder just to express its own frustration.

Eventually, I'd had enough. One day, after another morning of chemical warfare and the soundtrack of nail clippers,

I looked at her and said, "Pack your lotions and your nail files. This studio isn't big enough for both of us." She left, and the air cleared. But I didn't stick around to bask in my newfound solitude. I packed up too and moved into a three-bedroom house my brother-in-law, John, had rented outside of San Jose. The house was far more space than two men with questionable priorities needed, but we quickly turned it into a base for our misadventures. John and I dove headfirst into the Los Gatos nightlife, becoming regulars at bars like Black Watch and Last Call.

Drinking wasn't just a pastime—it was practically an Olympic sport. Nights blurred into bar tabs, flirting, and wild rides through the Santa Cruz Mountains on my Yamaha—drunk on Kamikaze, guts, and too many bets I somehow kept winning.

And then there was Kata a girl from Budapest.

We met online, back when digital dating was new, awkward, and just slightly less fake than it is now. For six months, we exchanged messages late into the night, convinced that I was already in love with this tall, blonde Hungarian woman I had never met.

When Kata finally decided to visit me, I was nervous. Could this really be the same person I'd been chatting with for half a year? Or was she some kind of elaborate internet prank? I jumped on my Yamaha and sped off to meet her at San Francisco airport, feeling like a cross between a knight on horseback and a lovesick fool.

And there she was, stepping out of the terminal. She didn't need an introduction. Kata was everything I'd imagined—long legs, a dazzling smile, and the kind of presence that made me forget how to breathe. I'm not saying there was a literal glow around her, but if angels were real, she was definitely part of their union. We hit it off right away, even though I was knee-deep in a party phase — the kind with loud music, late nights, and way too many empty bottles. Life at the three-bedroom house was a blur of laughter, hangovers, and ill-advised late-night food choices. But Kata shifted dynamic, fit right into our strange little setup, and the three of us shared the house for a few weeks.

John didn't mind—he seemed to enjoy the added company—but Kata and I soon realized we wanted a space of our own. That's when we made the full circle back to the same studio complex I had once shared with Simone. Only this time, it was a fresh start, free of citrus mists and clashing nail clippers.

Kata, for reasons I'll never understand, stuck around. She cleaned up after my messes and somehow turned everything into a home. Within weeks, it was clear she wasn't going back to Hungary anytime soon.

By the time we hit two years, we were inseparable. Kata calmed me in ways I didn't think were possible. And Patrick, the unlikeliest cupid, took credit for it all, insisting that his advice—and his steak recipes—had saved me.

Over the next decade, Kata and I shared countless adventures across the U.S., the kind of stories that could fill entire chapters on their own. But that's for later. For now, all you need to know is that I had found my partner, my calm in the storm, and someone who made even the wildest days worth it.

Looking back now, I wouldn't change a thing, every twist and turn led me to Kata.

And as far as gambles go, this one paid off in spades.

Syrah, Sunburn, and the Goddess in Flip-Flops

We didn't just arrive in Santa Ynez. We descended like outlaws, like Gypsy winos in a Cadillac DeVille with duct tape on the tail lights and half a mattress stuffed in the back seat. That car had seen things—Sequoia giants, Death Valley mirages, forgotten mining towns with rusty signs and desert rats selling moonshine in chipped mason jars. It coughed up oil like an old drunk spitting tobacco, but it never left us stranded.

And in the passenger seat, barefoot and radiant—Kata. My sun-charmed Valkyrie. Six feet of trouble with a laugh that could short-circuit satellites. Flip-flops dangling from her fingers, curls wild in the wind, lips stained with cherry ChapStick and defiance. Her feet, Jesus… they belonged in a museum. Perfect little works of Hungarian sculpture wrapped in Californian dust. I still don't know how a girl that elegant agreed to sleep with me in a car that smelled like spilled Merlot and burnt clutch.

We pitched our tent outside Solvang, in a campground that looked like the setting for a Danish horror flick—windmills, sunflowers, and feral squirrels that eyeballed us like we owed them rent. Bebel Gilberto played from our half-dead boombox while we sipped Rideau Syrah and chewed goat cheese like we were nobility slumming it.

"This cheese tastes like armpit," I said.

"Your armpit," Kata replied, grinning, tanned legs stretched out, eyes glassy with wine and freedom.

That's how we traveled. Cheap wine, shared smirks, zero plan. Drifters with expensive taste and no budget. We weren't tourists. We were fugitives from the ordinary, and Santa Ynez was just the next lucky hostage.

We started our wine rampage in Los Olivos, a one-street wonderland where every building is either a tasting room or pretending not to be. Kata wore a sundress that made rosé look jealous. People stared. Of course they did. She looked like the kind of woman who should've been helicoptered into Napa—not crawling vineyard-to-vineyard on a busted-up mountain bike next to a kitchen-scarred Hungarian lunatic.

At Arthur Earl, we sampled a Viognier that whispered peaches and second thoughts. Kata licked a drop from her wrist and said, "Too polite."

She liked her wines the way she liked her men—loud, dark, and likely to stain the sheets.

Next door, the tasting list at Alexander & Wayne read like a prayer. We downed eleven wines for six bucks, and by the time we got to the Zinfandel, the winemaker Louis showed up with a grin like the Marlboro Man's drunk cousin. He told us he hand-picks every grape. "Even the damn squirrels won't get to them first," he said, waving a leathery fist at the horizon.

Kata leaned in close, conspiratorial. "Tell him about Tokaji," she whispered. So I did. Told him about Szepsy's nectar of the gods, the Tokaji Eszencia thick enough to patch a roof tile. His eyes lit up. "Corner shop's got a five-puttonyos in gold wrap," he said, like he was giving us the map to El Dorado.

Of course we found it. The bottle sat like a jewel on the shelf, gleaming like home. The shop owner tried to pronounce "puttonyos" and failed spectacularly. Kata laughed so hard she snorted, and for a second, the whole shop was alive with the kind of joy you can't bottle.

We biked through Foxen Canyon in the heat of hell itself—sun above, fire trucks below, hawks overhead, and ash in the wind. The road shimmered like a lie, and the canyon stank of burnt oak and everything we couldn't afford to want.

By the time we hit Firestone Winery, we were sunburned, thirsty, and half-feral. But Kata? Still glowing. She could've walked into a Vogue shoot, dust and all. We tasted eleven wines and stole the crystal glasses—souvenirs of sin.

The last stop was Foxen, and they shut the doors at 4:00 p.m. sharp like they'd heard we were coming. Liability, sure—but really? They just didn't want two drunken Europeans giggling in the vines and scaring the influencers.

We coasted back to camp just as the sky turned violet. No selfies, no itinerary, just Syrah-stained teeth and shared silence. She curled up in the tent with her head on my chest, still laughing about the squirrel war in the vineyards. I looked around and thought, this is it. This is the wine-stained, sunburned American dream. And I'm living it with the most beautiful barefoot terrorist in the western hemisphere.

Kitchen Legend

Santa Monica, 2008.

I was skating a Sector 9 longboard, barefoot, one hand gripping a paper bag hiding the coldest beer I'd touched in days. Eric, from the grill station, cruised alongside me—shirtless, tattoos melting under the sun, already three sips ahead. We weren't talking. We were floating. Two burned-out kitchen dogs slicing past the palm trees like kids who'd escaped the institution for 24 golden hours.

We passed the beer back and forth as we rolled through Brentwood, the wind doing what the walk-in fridge never could—cooling the burn off our skin. My board? A gift from Nimród Antal himself. Director. Legend. Hand-delivered, duct-taped like contraband. A relic of freedom with soft wheels and a thousand stories in its grip tape. At a red light, we coasted to a stop. Nearby, someone was doing lunges with perfect form and zero joy. Eric took a sip, squinted sideways.

"You think Machiavelli's alive?"

I didn't answer Eric right away. The question wasn't if he was alive. It was how many people were still recovering. Nicholas Machiavelli wasn't just a chef. He was a kitchen-altering event. A walking system update delivered with knives and contempt. Tall. Gaunt. Inked from clavicle to jaw like a prison confession in progress. And always sweating. Not "working hard" sweat—pharmaceutical sweat. Synthetic. Tactical. His pores were trying to detox from a Berlin weekend he never talked about. He didn't walk into the kitchen. He materialized—already halfway through yelling at your prep, or already fixing it.

Mack hated mediocrity. He hated weak chefs. He hated your tweezers. He especially hated tasting spoons left in containers. I saw him throw one at a guy's foot once. Point first. The guy yelped like a kicked pug. His voice? Deep enough to shake the salamander shelf. And he didn't yell. He judged. Quietly. Terminally. You'd plate something. Slide it down the pass. And he'd just look at it—tilt his head like a crow spotting something shiny and disappointing—and say,

"...No."

Then he'd push it back toward you like it was radioactive.

Luc—remember Luc? The saucier from Marseille? Cried. Cried. Took his knives, his ego, and his lavender hand lotion and quit. On a Saturday. And Mack? Mack just said, "I wasn't that mean." He hated molecular gastronomy, "Sodium alginate?" he'd scoff. "You mean culinary fraud dust?" One time a stagiaire brought in a 'deconstructed coq au vin.' Mack picked it apart with a fork, sniffed it, tasted one dot of beet foam, and said, "If this bird could see what you did to it, it would fly into a power line out of shame." You want brutal?

Try watching someone explain sous-vide to Mack. The man who slow-braised lamb necks in cast iron like a medieval punishment. He didn't just mock it. He turned it into theatre. "You vacuum-packed meat like it's going to space. Congratulations. Now go sear something before I cry blood." He once sharpened his knife on the spine of a cleaver because someone borrowed his steel. He wasn't normal. He was useful. When shit hit the fan—and it always did—he'd just... appear. Shirt untucked. Eyes spinning. Voice low. "What station's bleeding?" You'd blink, and suddenly the fish was seared, the risotto tight, the plates clean. And Machiavelli would be wiping his blade with a rag that might've been a T-shirt yesterday. He didn't say goodbye. Never "good shift." Never "see you tomorrow." He'd just vanish.

One minute yelling at you for breaking the beurre blanc, next minute—gone. Into the walk-in? Out the back door? Into another dimension? Then two days later: boom. There he was. Same boots. Same flour-dusted pants. Same stare.

He wasn't friendly. He wasn't gentle. But every single one of us would've followed him into battle if he called. Because Nicholas Machiavelli didn't cook for applause. He cooked because it was his way of silencing the chaos. And when his music hit—some Eastern Bloc dance remix that sounded like a Soviet tractor factory falling in love—he'd start moving. Spinning. Gliding. Moonwalking past the fryer. Like a pop icon stuck in a kitchen.

One night—this is real, I swear on my last clean apron—some influencer showed up unannounced with a camera crew. Claimed she had a reservation. She didn't. Wanted gluten-free, dairy-free, nut-free... flavor-free. Mack stepped out from the back, wiping sweat off his forearms like he'd just hooked up with Emily—the waitress, frankly, distractingly sexy—in the broom closet next to the mop sink.

Which, to be fair, wasn't off the table. Same glazed expression. Same crooked grin. He smelled faintly of rosemary and something best left unspoken. Didn't say a word. Just looked at the camera, then at her, then back at the camera. Then—no warning—he picked up a parsnip, bit into it like an apple, and said,

"Tell kitchen is closed... spiritually." Turned around. Gone.

The whole dining room froze. Silence, like after someone pulls the pin but before the boom. The maître d' started blinking in Morse code. The influencer left. Her crew followed, dragging ring lights like corpses.

We served 93 covers that night. Perfect service. Not because we were pros. But because Mack had banished a demon.

Kitchen legend? Please. He was a myth with knife calluses. And as we coasted down San Vicente half-buzzed, reeking of SPF 15 and leftover shift sweat—we didn't say much. We were thinking the same thing anyway.

Mack was probably off somewhere slicing ribeye in a basement speakeasy or slow-roasting a goat in a parking garage.
Or dead. Either way, the kitchen felt empty without him. Less dangerous. Worse.

We still had our burns, our borrowed tricks, our irrational fear of garnishes.

And if we were smart—which we weren't—we'd hold onto the one thing Mack ever actually taught us:

Don't talk too much. Keep your knives sharp. And hope you learned enough not to burn the sauce.

The Road Through El Paso

By the year 2000, life in America had become a blur of road trips, national parks, and just enough drama to keep things interesting. Kata and I had crossed the country four times—north, south, coast to coast. Yosemite, Zion, Key Largo, the Redwoods. The van was home, the highways familiar.

This time, we were driving back to California from Florida—high hopes, full tank, the usual plan. But somewhere near El Paso, the freedom ran out. Not because the van broke down. That old thing purred like a cat. The problem came when we hit a border patrol checkpoint.

We'd barely handed over our IDs before the officer motioned us to pull over. Within minutes, we were surrounded, handcuffed, and herded into the back of a patrol vehicle that reeked of sweat, fear, and desperation. Every stop along the way added more detainees, each one with a face more defeated than the last. By the time the vehicle was full, the air inside was suffocating. I glanced at Kata, her pale face streaked with worry, and felt a deep pang of guilt. This wasn't what she'd signed up for.

When we arrived at what they called an "immigration holding camp," it became clear we were in for an extended stay. Kata's valid tourist visa wasn't enough to save her immediately. Until it could be confirmed by fax from the San Francisco immigration office, she was stuck in the same fluorescent-lit purgatory as the rest of us. Dressed in a jumpsuit like mine, she even had dinner in line with the other detainees—a surreal image that would stick with me. Finally, hours later, the fax arrived, and she was released—frazzled, exhausted, but free.

I wasn't so lucky. My two years of overstaying were enough to make me an official fugitive in their eyes. To make matters worse, they were convinced I wasn't Hungarian but Romanian, and the word "gypsy" hung in the air like an accusation. The days that followed were a mix of boredom, survival, and strange camaraderie. My cellmates were a ragtag group of South Americans and Russians, some of whom I bonded with over endless games of chess. The South Americans laughed through missing teeth, the Russians played like their lives depended on it, and I used my best moves to stay sane. Communication was a patchwork of gestures, broken English, and frustration.

The camp itself was another story. Privately owned and operated, its primary goal seemed to be profit. I learned that some of the inmates had been stuck there for over six months, forgotten by the system. They had no access to proper legal representation, no one asking questions on their behalf. The building functioned like a hotel—except one funded by the government, paying $120 per inmate per day. To ensure profitability, the camp had to stay full, which meant our care was as low-cost as possible. Meals were barely edible, and medical attention was limited to the bare minimum.

We were allowed outside for fresh air only once a day, for one hour. That single hour felt like salvation—a brief taste of freedom that made the rest of the day even harder to endure.

Eventually, after three long weeks inside that camp near El Paso, I walked free—thanks to my friend Khurrum, who posted an $1,800 bond. That bond was my ticket out, and Kata had been fighting like hell to get me there. She called the Hungarian embassy, hunted down contacts, pleaded with anyone who might listen. The phone line was her battleground, and somehow, she won.

Once I got out, we moved to New York. Started over. New city, new noise. But the case followed me like a bad smell. I still had to show up in court. The original venue was back in Texas, but I wasn't about to drive across the desert again just to face the same system that locked me up in the first place. And I sure as hell wasn't flying there. What if I got flagged, pulled aside, had to explain myself again? No thanks. So, we filed to move the case.

California felt safer. More lenient. Let's be honest—if you're an illegal immigrant trying to blend in, there are worse places to be than California. So the case was reassigned to San Francisco.

Now this was the year 2000. No fancy apps or streamlined immigration websites. If you wanted to understand how the system worked, you had to dig. I became obsessed with this one site: the Stein Report. Ugly layout. No colors. No filters. Just pure, uncut data—lists of border crossings, arrests, hearings. Who got caught, who got deported. It was the kind of truth you couldn't Google. I'd scroll for hours, copying anything that seemed important, like I was building my own survival manual.

When the day came, I flew out to San Francisco from New York, heart pounding through airport security. I made it. I showed up to the courtroom early, expecting a crowd. But the waiting room was dead. Just me and a Mexican family with four kids. I found my name taped to the door—big court list, maybe fifty names total. But nobody else came. Just me and that one family. That's how much people cared about immigration court. Or maybe they were just too scared to show up.

The guard opened the door, looked around like he expected a parade. Then he sighed. That was it for the day. The judge was gentle with the family. I was hopeful. Maybe I'd get lucky. But the second it was my turn, the mood shifted. The kindness disappeared. The words were cold, sharp, mechanical. I don't remember the exact phrasing, but it cut. I stood there, feeling like a criminal, a fool. I was declared guilty of overstaying and given four months to leave voluntarily.

Voluntary. What a word.

I nodded along, pretending to accept it, but deep inside I already knew—I wasn't going anywhere.

Back to Manhattan—straight back to the chaos that felt like safety. The city buzzed with life, neon nerves twitching on every street corner, yellow cabs snarling through intersections, steam hissing from underground like the city itself was trying to breathe. We slipped right back in like we'd never left. Invisible.

Kata took a job at Serafina in Midtown—hostessing for wealthy diners who pretended not to notice the accents. I worked nights. We rented a shoebox in Queens where the walls sweated during the summer, a humid tomb with the roar of the subway as a lullaby. It was life in a pressure cooker—no money, no papers, no guarantee of anything except noise.

Eventually, we made a move. A friend of a friend had a lead—a one-bedroom flat in Spanish Harlem, half a block from Central Park. The building was cracked but standing, and that was enough. The park was our backyard, the city our jungle. We were holding on, even if by the fingernails.

I took a job at Cinquanta on the Upper East Side. For all the kitchens I've cooked in, this was the darkest, filthiest hole of them all. A dungeon masquerading as a kitchen—crammed under a skylight that never worked and hidden behind a restaurant that looked halfway respectable. There were corners so pitch-black even the cockroaches moved with caution. No windows. No vents. The only oxygen came through the single front door—a weak gasp of air from the dining room.

The kitchen was a cauldron of tension, its heart a massive pot of tomato sauce bubbling like an angry red ocean—only it wasn't on a stove. It sat low to the ground, perched on a single, sputtering burner near the floor, forcing us to sidestep it like a landmine. Wrong place, wrong setup, but it boiled nonstop, like it knew it didn't belong and was pissed about it. The owner rarely set foot in the kitchen. He preferred to linger in the cramped dining area, standing around like a mafia don in exile—arms folded, counting money, basking in the sound of cutlery and submission. Everyone watched him, even when pretending not to. His arrogance filled the room like secondhand smoke. The staff worked in rigid silence, every move choreographed to avoid triggering another eruption. Giuliani once came in, sat facing the wall. Woman next to him watching the door like a bodyguard. They barely touched their food. Nobody went near them. That kind of silence doesn't ask—it orders.

Another time, Keanu Reeves walked in. Head down, fast—outrunning recognition—straight to the bathroom. Brushed past me like a jolt. Quiet, but heavy. Some people don't need to speak. The air does it for them.

The heat clung to everything—walls, skin, nerves. The noise never stopped. I endured it, but I never felt at home. New York wasn't my place. I belonged in California.

Adding to the drama was the Albanian hostess Angelina, a woman more femme fatale than front-of-house. In her mid-thirties, moving with the grace of a cat and the confidence of a runway model nobody asked for, she prowled outside the restaurant, expertly trapping tourists in her web. "Come, come! The best Italian food in New York!" she'd purr, waving them inside like a magician casting a spell. Her charm was impossible to resist, and the tourists, dazzled by her beauty and persuasion, followed her like moths to a flame.

There were whispers in the kitchen that she was sleeping with the owner. And honestly, the way his barking turned into purring the moment she walked in made it hard to argue. The best part? His actual wife was there every day too—posted behind the bar with the dead-eyed stare of a woman who'd survived ten years of his shouting and a lifetime of terrible decisions.

New York itself mirrored that kitchen—unforgiving, relentless, and humid beyond belief. Everything felt sticky, from the subway seats to the thick air that clung to your skin. September 11, 2001, began like any other day. We were on the roof of our Queens building when we saw it—the smoke rising from the World Trade Center. For a moment, the city fell silent, the usual cacophony replaced by a stunned stillness. The days that followed were a blur of grief and resilience. New York, always so vibrant and alive, carried a weight that felt impossible to lift. But the city pressed on, as it always does, and so did we.

We left New York dripping out in my rearview and shot back to California, hungry for something that didn't feel like slow death.

First stop: the Bay Area. I landed a spot at Saratoga Country Club, cooking side by side with Schriver—my old comrade from The Basin. We ran buffets big enough to drown a wedding party. But outside that uptight country club bubble, life was strangely perfect. Kata and I rented a second-floor place on Saratoga Avenue—redwood views, a heated pool, and squirrels who treated the balcony like an Olympic vaulting event. No respect for gravity. No respect for us either.

The patio was a monster. Room for twenty-five, easy. We grilled everything out there—ribs, burgers, fish. That apartment witnessed more meat, joy, and red wine than most kitchens in Paris.

A 1970 Spitfire. Faded paint. Oil leaks. Personality in spades. It shouldn't have run—but it did. Loudly.

Cheflaszlo.com came together the way most things did back then—fast, scrappy, and just chaotic enough to stick.

Kata and I threw it up between work, snapping shots of farmers' markets and scribbling menus that promised exactly what I stood for: clean, simple, honest food. Market ingredients. Grandma's soul. Plated with some finesse and none of the pretension. No tweezers. No foams. No lab tricks. Just food that tasted like someone gave a damn. Because I did.

Somewhere between the holding cell in El Paso and the rooftop smoke of 9/11, I changed. The kid from Hungary who once begged for scraps in a border camp was now carving duck for billionaires in Beverly Hills.

From there, I slipped into private estates—cooking for athletes with trophy wives, politicians with skeleton closets, and celebrities who couldn't tell duck confit from chicken nuggets. These jobs weren't about food—hell no. They were about delivering the impossible, pretending it was effortless, and eating your pride for dessert.

After a few years of carving scars across the Bay Area, I packed my knives and moved south—chasing bigger sharks in Los Angeles, where the money was thicker and the egos somehow even thinner. It all kicked off there. Brent Sopel, for example—one of my early gigs. Before long, I became one of the most sought-after private chefs around. Why? Because I hunted down ingredients even the rich couldn't find in restaurants or stores. That was my whole philosophy: cook with better ingredients than money usually buys.

Through it all, Kata was still there—my partner in crime, the only steady beat in a world that spun faster every damn day.

The Art of the Hopper

Some chefs build their careers on discipline and loyalty, staying in one place long enough to have a dish named after them. Some!

Laszlo already had two paying jobs in San Jose. Two. But every other day, he'd climb into a dying Cadillac and cruise two and a half hours to Napa just to work for free at The French Laundry. No paycheck. No gas money. Just the privilege of being allowed to julienne vegetables near greatness.

It was grueling. Ridiculous. Insane.

But that's the price of proximity. You did it for the air—the same oxygen breathed by Michelin stars. You did it to stand elbow-to-elbow with culinary legends, hoping something would rub off—sauce technique, plating finesse, god-tier discipline, anything.

And in the end, it was all worth it for the one sentence he could drop for the rest of his life, anywhere, anytime: "Yeah... I worked at The French Laundry."

It all started 1997 in Budapest, at Gundel, Hungary's most iconic restaurant. Up-nose chefs, each competing in a cutthroat ballet of egos and while the atmosphere was far from friendly, it undeniably pushed the quality of the food to astonishing heights. I couldn't decide if I was impressed or terrified. Somehow, I managed to get a tour, probably because one of them mistook me for someone important. The highlight? A mushroom sauce bubbling in a stockpot the size of a Fiat, four chefs orbiting it like satellites locked in a gravy trance.

Belcanto sat in the shadow of the Budapest Opera House. The seafood was the star here — cling-film wrapped and poached to perfection, shockingly fresh for a landlocked country. The chef, a man with a jawline sharp enough to slice tuna, moved with the kind of precision that made you wonder if he'd trained with a scalpel. He claimed he had no time for small talk — but the moment there was an audience, he couldn't resist putting on a show.

In California, my hopping adventures truly took off.

Viaggio 1998 (Saratoga): I was here to spy, the owner of Le Mouton Noir, spineless as he was, sent me to poke around and report back. It was like a bad spy movie, only with less tuxedos and more lobster tails.

Basin 1999 (Saratoga): A fresh concept in a lively street where restaurants were locked in fierce competition for customers. The kitchen was run by a young, city-trained chef who was half visionary, half maniac. Signs like "DID YOU ICE THE FISH???" were plastered everywhere, a constant reminder of the horrors of rotten seafood. From mashed potatoes to meatloaf, I learned the kind of everyday brilliance that makes comfort food unforgettable, the bar staff invaded for their supplies tested my patience.

The Left Bank, 1999–2000 (Santana Row, San Jose): This was the Hopper jackpot. A French brasserie with a killer concept — the entire kitchen was exposed, a full-contact culinary show with nowhere to hide. Flames flared, steel clanged, and guests watched it all from a few feet away. I never met Chef Roland Passot, but his presence was felt in every detail — in the discipline, the plating, the tempo. Each station was its own universe, and the whole place moved like a machine with a soul. I left with a full notebook and a head full of ideas — and a new respect for chefs who cook with an audience.

Stanford University, Schwab Center 2000: Catering for the elite. Imagine serving lobster and filet mignon to thousands of people while thinking, what a waste of money. This was high-end catering on steroids, a whirlwind of extravagance.

The French Laundry 2000: The holy grail of fine dining. Standing in the same kitchen as culinary gods was surreal, but let's be honest—it felt like I was miles away from actually being a part of it. Still, I soaked in the atmosphere, saw things I couldn't unsee (in the best way), and paid more to get there than I care to admit.

231 Ellsworth 2001 (Menlo Park): This one deserves better than my foggy memory. My old friend Bill from the Plumed Horse gave me enormous attention here. He treated me like royalty who didn't deserve the title. I had the best "free lunch" for the work I put in, though the generosity made it feel like I owed him nothing. Bill, if you're reading this, get in touch—I owe you more than just gratitude.

La Cachette 2005 (Los Angeles): A brilliant jump. But the true gem in L.A. was Melisse 2008, where I learned the art of audacity. One day, I walked in unannounced, asked to see Chef Citrin, and to my shock, he came out. We spoke ten minutes. He fed me a three-course lunch—a complete stranger!—and by the next day, I was in. It wasn't just the food that stood out; it was the trust. I could stand anywhere in the kitchen, any time I wanted, even during the busiest moments. Stand and watch, stand and help—it didn't matter. Citrin's kitchen was an open book, and he let me read every page, plenty remained his secret.

The Alchemy of Fire and Steel

Los Angeles had its fair share of temples — Hollywood for the wannabes, Silicon Beach for the tech bros, and then there was La Cachette. No sign out front. No neon bullshit. If you didn't already know, you didn't belong. It was the crucible — where cooks either got forged into hardened steel or flamed out like cheap sauté pans left on high heat, under a kitchen clock stuck at 'too fucking late.' Time moved differently in that kitchen — heavy, humid, pulsing with bone stock and the leftover heat of cooks who hadn't quit yet. The low hum of discipline broken only by the snap of knives on wood and the occasional scream of a pan hitting the deck.

The one commanding the whole place? Chef Magnus "The Bear" Thorne, a man who could ruin your week with one look. If he said your sauce was too loose, it was already in the trash before you finished blinking. You didn't survive in this kitchen. You endured.

5:30 AM. The alley behind La Cachette was already alive.

Delivery vans idled, their exhaust mixing with the stale stink of last night's garbage. The back door cracked open, and Bililies—gaunt, silent, looking like he hadn't eaten in a decade—stepped out like a Roman emperor deciding who lived and who died.

Moulard duck from Sonoma? Passed. Hokkaido scallops, still pulsing under their shells? Barely.

Langoustines from Maine, still twitching? Fine.

Then came the tomatoes.

The produce guy held his breath. Bililies gave them one sniff, one squeeze — rejected. No words. Just a flick of the wrist. The driver muttered a quiet "Merde" and loaded the crates back onto the truck. He knew better than to argue.

Only the flawless made it in. Everything else went back — to the farmers' markets, the weekend warriors, the half-blind butchers pretending to be chefs.

By 7 AM, the morning brigade assembled—six chefs, sleeves rolled, eyes dead, fingers moving like they were wired to an unseen metronome. No greetings. No small talk.

Knives flashed, heat screamed off the burners, and hands moved like there was no plan B. Sofía, pastry wizard from Mexico City, tempered chocolate like she was defusing a bomb. Dario, ex-boxer turned butcher, deboned a suckling pig in under three minutes, hand rolled tobacco hanging from his lip. Lee, the sous-chef, never forgot a single order, a single request, or a single mistake. Ever.

At noon, the staff meal arrived—two massive pizzas from a hole-in-the-wall down the street, a battered pan of brownies. No plates, no napkins. Eat fast, eat standing. Someone passed around a bottle of Mexican salsa so evil it could strip paint. This was the only time the machine exhaled.

By 1 PM, the transition began. The night's menu hit the table. Bililies frowned. "The word 'poached' appears twice. One has to go." No argument. No discussion. One dish stayed poached, the other became confit.

From locked cabinets came La Cachette's secret weapons: Aged bordelaise reductions, Clarified consommés so clear you could read through them, Hand-harvested fleur de sel in tiny glass jars, duck liver mousse, pressed through a tamis like it was an Olympic event. By 3:30 PM, Nick, the expeditor, a caffeinated Zen monk with a stopwatch for a soul, slid in to run the final kitchen meeting. Service was coming, the frenzy begins.

5 PM. First tickets roll in. The kitchen ignites. Pans hit burners. Fingers move through mise en place with the precision of habit and the panic of time slipping. The roar of the hood vents drowns out anything resembling a rational thought. Orders crash down the line, tickets pouring out like a goddamn casino payout. Dario plates a Wagyu ribeye with black garlic purée.

"Garnish! Where the fuck is my garnish?!"

"Coming, coming!" Sofía dives in, micro-cilantro in hand, placing it like she's handling a Fabergé egg.

Chef Thorne is everywhere and nowhere.

He catches every flaw, every mistake, every half-assed attempt at excellence.

One line cook sends out a scallop that's been on the heat two seconds too long.

Without a word, Thorne flicks the plate against the wall. Shatters. "Redo it. You're better than that." No rage. No screaming. Just expectation. This wasn't a place for egos. This was a place for gods and their disciples.

11 PM. The last plates are sent. The final guests sip espresso, pick at their Grand Marnier soufflés. The kitchen, once a roaring battlefield, falls into silence. But it's not over. Stations scrubbed. Counters wiped. The smell of lemon bleach fights a losing battle against the ghosts of seared duck fat and black truffle. Chef Thorne gathers the crew. "Good service tonight. Tomorrow, we do better." And then, without another word, he disappears into his office.

The brigade exhales. Some light cigarettes. Others pour illicit shots of bourbon into battered coffee cups. A few, like Dario, just collapse onto an overturned crate and stare at the ceiling.

Tomorrow, it all happens again. And they'll be ready.

LA RAW

Central Ave and East 4th St. Fish market, at 3:00 a.m. Be sharp!

Forklifts shrieked backwards, pallets slammed into wet concrete, and boxes of Styrofoam and crushed ice burst open like carcasses. Wind slashed through the open bays—cold enough to crack your knuckles if you forgot your gloves. It smelled like salt, rust, and the belly of the Pacific—a mix that didn't wash off, no matter how hard you scrubbed.

It was already buzzing. Forklifts spun like angry wasps. One second of hesitation and you'd end up flattened against a pallet of sea urchin. Chefs hugged the shadows, scouting their prey.

But these weren't just any chefs. These were killers from Spago, Matsuhisa, Providence, Urasawa—the gods of LA's culinary Olympus. They came for perfection. One bad cut, one spoiled scallop, and your name vanished from the reservation list. Reputation here was more fragile than toro belly.

And they weren't here for California rolls. They wanted miracles in flesh, before the gate opens 7 for the public:

Geoduck Clam—the ugliest mollusk you'll ever see. Six kilos of meat with a grotesque, stretching neck. But once sliced into sashimi? It transformed—pearly, translucent, delicately crisp. They called it Mirugai on menus so customers wouldn't run screaming.

Santa Barbara Spot Prawns—alive when ordered, torched for ten seconds, butterflied, plated with crispy tempura made from their own heads. Sweeter than lobster, but sensitive as hell. Twenty-four hours out of water and they turn to mush. Chefs fished them from tanks like snipers selecting targets.

Uni—sea urchin, that velvet-briny paradox. Hacked out of black, spiky shells, golden roe gleaming like treasure. The French smear it on toast. The Japanese cradle it on rice and whisper its name. Most Americans just pretend to like it.

Unagi—sweetwater eel from Japan's Hamana River. The elite cut. Steamed, boned, grilled over charcoal, and painted with kabayaki sauce until it sizzles like a jazz solo. Japanese eat it for strength in the summer heat. LA just eats it to feel special.

And towering above them all: Bluefin Tuna. Toro. The belly of the beast—and that's what I was hunting.

Saul Guzman, tuna whisperer from Tuna Express, just a short walk away, once told me in a freezing back-alley fish vault on Stanford Street: "No one wanted fatty tuna before. Now? Toro, toro, toro. Even the Japanese are outbidding us."

He specialized in Canadian wild and Spanish farm-raised. "The yen's strong," he shrugged. "Always is."

They dragged 300-kilo monsters across the icy floor with meat hooks. Steam hissed where frozen skin met the warm air. A few swift cuts and the belly rolled away like satin muscle. The bones cracked. The waste hit the bin. The filets were wrapped like stolen art.

I watched a crew eat breakfast on the floor. Chopped bluefin on paper bags, lemon, Tabasco, torn bread, jalapeños. Latin sushi. They sat on crates, laughed, and ripped into fish that would sell for $60 a slice by dinner.

"Come back Monday," Saul told me. "You'll see hundreds laid out at once." By sunrise, it was all gone. Nods closed deals. No receipts. No second chances. This was the true battlefield of fine dining—where Michelin stars were earned before your first guest sat down.

That night, I entered Matsuhisa like I was walking into a dojo.

Behind the counter stood a quiet samurai in white. No wasted motion. No menu. Just a glance, a nod, a gesture. He handed me a piece of nigiri.

Toro—fatty tuna—melted on my tongue like raw velvet. Scallop curled into pickled ginger. Rice whispered with vinegar. You don't eat sushi like that. You receive it. It doesn't fill you—it transforms you.

And somewhere between bites, I realized: This wasn't Japanese anymore. This was LA. This was pop sushi—reborn in neon and yoga pants.

Ichiro Mashita, 1964. Corner of San Pedro and 2nd. They ran out of tuna. Subbed in avocado. Rolled it with crab and cucumber. California Roll. From there: Philadelphia. Rainbow. Spicy tuna. Dragon scale plating. Deep-fried cream cheese monstrosities. Tokyo made sushi. Los Angeles made it cool.

By midnight, I was outside again, belly full, brain fogged. The taxi driver turned his entire head to get a good look at me.

"Of course I know Matsuhisa," he barked, gravel voice, eyes sharp. "One Michelin star. One of the best we've got." He raised his index finger like a man who'd once stabbed someone for less.

"But you…" he said, jabbing it at my face, "…you need to go to Urasawa. Just got its second Michelin star. Only place you'll get shabu-shabu."

"Next time," I lied. (Truth? I had no idea what shabu-shabu was. And I couldn't afford it even if I sold my knives.)

He turned back forward. Silence. Then he whispered, like it was sacred: "Foie Gras with scallops."

We inched through Sunset like molasses. Outside Whisky a Go Go, two Jessica Simpson clones tottered across in fur coats, brushing against the cab. Punk kids smoked and loitered like characters in a Bukowski poem. The city didn't sleep—it twitched.

"Matsuhisa…" the cabbie sighed. "You'll enjoy it. But Urasawa…"

His voice drifted. He was gone. Dreaming. Savoring. Tasting something I couldn't afford, served on porcelain, eaten with reverence.

Then we hit La Cienega. He braked hard, slapped the meter, and called back softly:

"Itadakimasu."

Let's eat. Let's receive.

Let's worship the thing that died for us to feel alive.

The Culinary Crossroads

After years of navigating the high-octane kitchens, I found myself at a pivotal juncture. I had the knife skills of a samurai and the stamina of a marathon runner. But the knowledge level of those Michelin-star psychopaths? That was something else. Could I have reached it? Maybe. Did I want to? Absolutely not. What I really wanted was a decent life with Kata—more free time, more income, and something didn't require 16-hour shifts where I'd get screamed at for chopping chives "too emotionally."

Enter Diana, a wealthy woman in Pacific Palisades, whose Craigslist ad changed everything. Diana wasn't looking for a chef. She needed an assistant in her busy life, someone to oversee the staff, make sure the gardeners weren't growing a weed empire, and, occasionally, throw together a party spread. The best part? Weekends off, which meant time for freelance gigs, restaurant-hopping, and not collapsing in a walk-in fridge from exhaustion.

Diana wasn't exactly known for wild parties — but rich people don't need a reason. And since I was already standing in her ridiculously expensive kitchen, she figured: why not make me cook? That's how I ended up plating dinner for Anne Heche and Roseanne Barr. Cooking for A-listers isn't about reinventing the wheel — it's about effortless perfection. You take what they already love, and you elevate it without making a scene. No fireworks. No ego. Just pristine ingredients and food that whispers, yes, you're better than everyone else.

Their house was a fortress of steel and glass, hanging like a crown off the edge of the Palisades cliffs — earthquake-proof, ocean-view, and packed with paintings so expensive they could've bailed out a collapsing economy. Out back, the garden was its own strange kingdom: a perfect swimming pool framed by full-sized bronze monk statues, their weathered patina making them look like ancient relics dug up from some lost civilization.

The setup worked. It gave me the freedom to build my name as a private chef — and a front-row seat to the beautiful insanity of the ultra-rich. But working 40 hours a week for Diana was just one piece of the puzzle.

Kata and I were still figuring things out. We'd lived in New York, crammed into shoebox apartments, grinding impossible hours. We escaped the only way we knew how: endless road trips — Lake Tahoe, Death Valley, Vegas (five times), four full cross-country drives. And through it all, I stayed obsessed. Visiting cheesemakers and vineyards in Sonoma and Napa. Skating through Santa Monica on my skateboard, hunting down the perfect brown rice sushi. Thinking about food 24/7 — even while pumping diesel in the middle of nowhere.

A Glimpse Into Private Chef Life: Im in Beverly Hills, cooking for a family insanely rich. Their estate a self-sustaining ecosystem hidden in the middle of one of the wealthiest zip codes in the world. Their sprawling garden was essentially a working farm. Eight South American gardeners tended to every fruit, vegetable, and herb they consumed, working full time. Their private menagerie included roosters, hens, ducks, goats, mini pigs, rabbits, quails, turtles, and even goldfish ponds. Not to mention stables, three dogs, and several cats.

Before I cooked, I toured the garden. The head gardener advised me on what was freshest, explaining that the family almost never shopped at grocery stores. Their diet was strict—no dairy, no bread, no flour, no chocolate, no sweets, no red meat. Instead, they consumed a high-end pescatarian diet, with fresh seafood flown in from the East Coast and Alaska, stored in seventeen refrigerators scattered throughout the estate. Seventeen refrigerators. I counted. Twice.

They were the kind of family that still believed food should be slow, intentional, and meaningful. It showed me that, even in one of the most fast-paced cities in the world, people could still live by old-world values. And it made me reflect on my own past—growing up in Hungary, where most of us ate healthier without even realizing it. Back then, our food wasn't fast or processed. It was grown in small gardens, poultry was raised in backyards, and milk, butter, and sour cream came from the family cow. It wasn't luxury. It was just life. And that's when I realized—I had carved out a new path. I wasn't working for a restaurant anymore. I was working for the top 1% in their own homes.

The Montgomery residence was a marvel of design and innovation. Perched on a bluff overlooking the Pacific, it wasn't just another Malibu mansion—it was a sanctuary of thoughtful luxury. Crosby Ross, the visionary designer behind the home, had created something extraordinary. The centerpiece was a reverse-pressure vacuum system that directed airflow out toward the sea. This ingenious feature allowed the owners to throw open the windows and doors, welcoming the light and sound of the ocean, while ensuring the salty breeze couldn't wreak havoc on the pristine, high-end furniture.

The owners, two impeccably kind gentlemen who worked as bookkeepers, shared a bond as unique as their home. With their daughter—a beautiful product of modern science and both their DNA—they created an environment filled with warmth, humor, and an appreciation for the finer things in life. Cooking for them wasn't just a job; it was an invitation into a world where generosity and hospitality were paramount.

My connection to the Montgomery residence began with a single dinner and grew into countless evenings of culinary exploration. They loved hosting, and I became a fixture at their gatherings, whether for intimate family meals or extravagant soirées. The pinnacle of these events was the legendary 11-course dinner—a feast so grand that it still stands out as one of the most ambitious undertakings of my career. The preparation for that evening was meticulous. Every detail had to be perfect, from the custom table settings to the luxurious linens—linens so fine that the dry cleaning bill alone topped $700.

Crosby Ross, the designer of the Montgomery residence, was not just a client—he was a patron of my craft. A true connoisseur, Crosby understood that food, like design, was an experience meant to evoke emotion. I cooked for him and his partner countless times, whether for their personal enjoyment or to dazzle their clients. Whenever Crosby completed one of his stunning multi-million-dollar homes, he would call on me to prepare a feast for the new homeowners—a grand gesture of welcome. These gigs introduced me to a world of clients who valued not just luxury, but the artistry behind it.

Sadly, the Montgomery residence no longer stands. The recent Palisades fire took it, along with so many memories. Seeing the news of the flames swallowing the home was sad—not just for the loss of the structure, but for the laughter, love, and stories that had unfolded within its walls.

For those of us who work in luxury, we move through these perfectly curated spaces, we serve in them, we create memories in them. But at the end of the day, we don't own them. We are guests in a world of excess.

The Big Decision – Leaving the USA (Like It Never Happened)

Kata and I had tried to have kids, but biology wasn't on our side.

After some medical interventions that didn't work, we faced reality and made another big decision—to leave the U.S. But leaving wasn't as simple as booking a flight and waving goodbye at JFK.

We had been living in the U.S. for nearly a decade on an expired visa—fully off the grid, no social security, no official records—just two well-fed phantoms slipping between the cracks.

So, when the time came to go, we didn't need to disappear—we just needed to walk away. And that's exactly what we did.

We voluntarily departed, packed our lives into backpacks, and walked across the southern border into Mexico, launching into a seven-week backpacking trip through Latin America. Why? Because Budapest offered something the U.S. never could: three rounds of in-vitro fertilization (IVF) for free. Meanwhile, in America, just one attempt cost more than a decent home—and that was before the hidden fees, unnecessary tests, and the emotional surcharge of dealing with U.S. healthcare bureaucracy.

So, we had a plan:

-Leave the U.S. quietly, without a trace.
-Wander through Latin America like lost, sweaty explorers.
-Get to Hungary, try IVF, and see if science could do what nature refused to.

And after that? Malta, where a new adventure (our own restaurant called Tal Latini) was waiting.

But first, we had to survive weeks of questionable bus rides, bizarre meals, and Carlos-level chaos in the wilds of Central and South America.

The FBI, and a One-Way Ticket Out

Before Laszlo left the United States, he had already made a name for himself—whether he meant to or not. For nearly a decade, he had cooked for celebrities, sports icons, ambassadors, and politicians, crafting menus with ingredients so exclusive that some clients probably thought they had been hand-harvested by Tibetan monks under the light of a full moon.

Among his more extravagant culinary weapons were:

Banyu Banyu nuts (because regular nuts were for peasants) Abalone (a mollusk so rare that its price tag came with an apology) Tasmanian crayfish (because normal lobsters lacked mystery) Pinctada Maxima pearl meat (a cross between scallops and prawns, harvested from the same mussels that produce some of the world's most expensive pearls) King George whiting, roasted in paperbark (because aluminum foil is for amateurs) Pepe Saya butter infused with kombu essence (so luxurious, it practically deserved its own security detail) Norwegian reindeer meat, paired with wild lingonberries (Rudolph, look away) Tsar Caviar, harvested nearby, plated like diamonds for breakfast.

His ability to turn these ingredients into edible masterpieces had earned him a loyal, high-net-worth clientele. It even caught the attention of the Malibu Times, which once wrote:

"Raised in a pastoral town in Southern Lake Balaton, Hungary, Laszlo trained in the best restaurants in Europe and New York and has served as private chef to ambassadors and movie stars. Whether you are vegan or a lover of Foie

Gras, Cheflaszlo will redefine the concept of fine dining in the comfort of home."

Not a bad headline for a guy who had once burned an omelet in his mother's kitchen.

But as it turned out, food wasn't the only thing that put him in the spotlight.

The FBI Case That No One Saw Coming: Long before Laszlo had any intention of making headlines, he had somehow managed to help the FBI catch an international con artist. Yes, really.

A notoriously slick fraudster named Kafashian-Legaspi had been scamming his way across the U.S., dodging authorities with the grace of a man who had watched too many bad crime movies. The FBI had spent years trying to track him down.

They failed.

And then, by pure accident, they stumbled upon Laszlo's website, SuperRipoff.com, a website dedicated to exposing Kat.. A woman named Kat hired the chef for a last-minute birthday dinner, then paid with a fake $1,300 check. Thanks of SuperRipoff.com, the authorities were able to trace the scammer's whereabouts, leading to his eventual arrest.

The Los Angeles Times even ran a full feature on the case, highlighting how, without Laszlo's website, the fraudster might still be out there swindling innocent people and pretending to be someone important.

So there it was—after years of fine dining, Michelin-level meals, and carefully curated menus, his biggest contribution to America was... accidentally catching a conman.

Figures.

Lights, Camera, Chef – The Documentary: As if the FBI story weren't enough, Laszlo soon found himself under a very different kind of media spotlight.

A Hungarian film crew from Határtalan Emberek (People Without Boundaries) reached out with a surprising request:

They wanted to fly to Los Angeles and film a documentary about his life. The producers wanted to highlight successful Hungarians living abroad, and somehow, he had made the list.

So, with cameras rolling, they followed him through the cutthroat, high-pressure world of private cheffing for the ultra-rich. They documented it perfectly—people willing to drop ten grand on a meal, only to fixate on the smallest details. Fine dining wasn't about pleasure anymore. It was about control.

By the time the documentary wrapped, one thing became clear: This was his legacy in America. A 30-minute feature film that captured a decade of high-stakes, high-pressure, high-net-worth cooking madness.

And Then… We Walked Away

Just weeks after the cameras stopped rolling, Laszlo and Kata packed their lives into backpacks, walked across the southern border, and vanished into Latin America.

No farewell parties. No dramatic goodbyes. Just a quiet exit, the way they had entered.

The next chapter would begin with seven weeks of questionable bus rides, bizarre meals, and occasional brushes with disaster. They weren't just leaving the U.S. They were erasing themselves from it.

Escape from California, Straight into the Fire

We left California in a hurry—maybe too much of a hurry. Ten years had vanished like a fever dream, slipping away before we even had time to process it. What remained? Eighty boxes of belongings, packed up and loaded into a shipping container, bound for Hungary, floating across the ocean like our past life drifting away. And yet, we didn't feel light. We were carrying something heavier—memories, emotions, and the nagging realization that leaving a place isn't as simple as just walking away.

The hardest moment came right after we crossed the border. There we stood, already on the other side, just meters from the checkpoint, staring back in silence at the golden California hills—the very hills we had called home just moments before.

A whirlwind of emotions hit us all at once. Excitement, because we were finally embarking on our long-planned South American adventure. Fear, because we had no idea what awaited us when, after all our travels, we would land at Ferihegy Airport and step back into a country we hadn't lived in for a decade. And then, out of nowhere, a gut punch I hadn't expected—not even Machu Picchu could wash it away.

Homesickness.
It hit like a horse kick to the chest—far stronger than what I'd felt ten years earlier when I left my actual homeland.

We shared a quick round of sentimental hugs, heaved our human-sized backpacks onto our shoulders, and crossed the parking lot to the bus station. The bus was leaving in half an hour, heading south.

The Fastest Trip Through Mexico (With No Sightseeing Included):

Let me get this out of the way: we barely saw Mexico—and yes, I know how embarrassing that sounds. Our friend, Iván Sárecz, who had spent months joyfully wandering the country, couldn't understand why we were barreling through it at breakneck speed. But the explanation was simple: we had exactly three days to get to Mexico City, where our flight (through Costa Rica) would take us to Lima, Peru.

So, as much as it pains me to admit it, Yucatán, El Pinacate, and the ruins of the Maya civilization wouldn't be on the itinerary. But don't worry—what we did experience was more than enough to write about for days. Because we spent forty-five miserable hours on that godforsaken dirty, broken-down, smoke-filled bus. And that was just the beginning.

We Are Not Hardcore Backpackers (Let's Get That Clear):

Before I go any further, let me make something very clear: I am not some tough, seasoned, adventure-seeking, hostel-loving backpacker. Neither is Kata. Sure, I've travelled plenty. But before this trip, I had never spent weeks eating garbage, dodging drug-searching soldiers, or trying to sleep in a bed that probably had more fleas than actual mattress foam.

I was not used to cold showers. Shared, filthy dorm rooms. Random military checkpoints where armed men (and their dogs) sniff through your belongings. The unbearable stench of unwashed humans in an enclosed space. Eating questionable, weeks-old slop. At first, it was hell. But strangely, after about three weeks, I stopped noticing most of it. I even—dare I say it—started to enjoy the madness. But until then? Pure suffering.

Meet Carlos: Our Bus Driver (and Shady Desert Navigator):

Let's just go ahead and name our bus driver Carlos. I'll be mentioning him a lot, so it's only practical to give him a name. (Let's be honest—if you're picturing a sweaty, wild-eyed southern bus driver named Carlos, you're already halfway there.) Carlos was a legend in his own right. The journey was supposed to take forty hours. It ended up being forty-five hours of pure agony. And honestly? It could have been even longer—but Carlos had zero regard for legalities, road rules, or human decency.

Take the border crossing, for example. Instead of stopping in Ensenada to get us the necessary Mexican entry permits, Carlos just slowed down at the checkpoint, rolled down the window, and handed over a thick wad of pesos to the uniformed officer. The soldier glanced at the cash, nodded, and waved us through.

And that was just the first checkpoint. At least twenty more times, we woke up in the middle of the night to find our bus surrounded by armed soldiers and drug-sniffing dogs. But Carlos? He just casually slipped some cash to the guards and kept driving.

The "Fine Dining" Experience on a Moving Trash Can

To his credit, Carlos knew his way around Mexican roadside food stalls. He only stopped at places that wouldn't kill us (immediately, at least). The food was shockingly good—but the violent diarrhea afterward was less enjoyable.

One time, Carlos stopped in the middle of nowhere, ran into a half-collapsed, roofless shack, and disappeared for twenty minutes. When he came back, he was beaming with joy, carrying an empty blue ice chest. What was in it before? I didn't ask. Because, frankly, I didn't want to know.

Carlos Redeems Himself (Sort of):

Carlos, for all his moral failings, did one thing right. Somewhere near Tepic, he stopped at a dust-covered village and introduced us to the best tortilla of our lives. An old woman, working in a crumbling roadside shack, made them by hand right in front of us. She kneaded the dough, rolled it out, and cooked each tortilla fresh on the griddle. We devoured them like starving wolves. The meat inside? Unidentifiable. A giant pot of floating, gelatinous chunks of mystery flesh simmered in its own fat, and I decided not to ask questions. But the tortillas? Heavenly. Soft, warm, and perfect.

Carlos got one good point for that stop. And the old woman? We practically kissed her hands in gratitude. Final Thoughts: Misery, Madness, and One Perfect Meal. Looking back, I realize now: this was only the beginning.

We were still soft, still complaining, still clinging to the idea that travel should be comfortable. But this bus ride? It started to break us in. By the end of the trip, I wouldn't be phased by cold showers, flea-ridden mattresses, or sleeping next to armed drug dealers. But at that moment? It was pure hell.

We had a handheld GPS, a small miracle of technology, bought back in the U.S. before our trip. It wasn't perfect—it only displayed major cities—but at least it showed our direction, altitude, and how far we were from the next big town. That information was only slightly comforting as we sat in a filthy, freezing bus, somewhere between Hermosillo, Los Mochis, Culiacán, Mazatlán, and Guadalajara, inching our way toward Mexico City on what felt like a never-ending road trip from hell. By this point, we had been traveling for two full days and nights without proper hygiene.

Our necks were stiff from the awful seats, which had no headrests, making sleep impossible. But, as it turned out, sleep deprivation was the least of our problems.

Because Carlos, our fearless, reckless bus driver, was in the process of setting a new world record for "longest time driving without rest." For reasons unknown (but likely financial), Carlos refused to let the backup driver take over. He drove for 12 to 16 hours straight, barely resting, and the one time he did lie down, it was under the bus, curled up with the luggage, for maybe 20 minutes. That meant we were being chauffeured through the Mexican desert by a dangerously sleep-deprived man, whose main goal in life seemed to be surviving the trip without ever stopping for sleep, sanity, or basic human decency.

If it wasn't the rock-hard seats ruining our night, it was the subzero air-conditioning, which had turned the bus into a rolling icebox. And if neither of those did it, then it was Carlos himself, who was slowly but surely falling asleep at the wheel. At some point, Kata started watching him in the rearview mirror. "His blinks are getting slower," she whispered. I looked up. She was right. His eyes were closing longer than they should.

He must have realized we were watching him because he angled the mirror so we couldn't see his face anymore. That was not reassuring. We sat there, in the pitch-black night, knowing that at any moment, we could be launched off the road into a fiery death. Instead of panicking, we did what any rational person would do: We started joking about it.

"Well," I said, "if we go down, there's no unfinished business. No letters to write, no revenge plots. Just splatter and silence."

Kata nodded. "Yep, this is it. This is the bus that came for us. It waited for us to finish a chapter of our lives, and now it's taking us straight to the afterlife." The only thing that ruined the illusion was the peaceful snoring of the other passengers. Carlos, however, was not peacefully snoring.

The Bathroom Situation (Or: How to Suffer with Dignity):

If I had to rank the worst parts of this trip, the bathroom situation is very high on the list. Carlos, our beloved leader, never once cleaned the onboard toilet. Keep in mind, this was a bus full of men—the details are not necessary, but let's just say I discovered my flexibility was not nearly as advanced as I had once thought. How Kata managed? I don't know, and I don't want to know.

Mexico Through a Filthy Bus Window:

For days, all we saw was poverty, dust, and endless piles of trash. Even far from towns, there was garbage everywhere—as if civilization had extended its reach, but only as far as leaving waste behind. Collapsed houses with no roofs or doors. Crumbling brick walls with nothing behind them. Small children sitting on broken car seats, staring blankly at passing traffic. And dogs. Dozens of starving, skeletal stray dogs, chasing buses, scavenging for anything edible. We threw our leftover food out the window, but it was heartbreaking to see how long it took them to trust it. They would sniff it, poke it with their noses, as if they couldn't believe humans would actually give them food.

The 2 AM Nightmare in Guadalajara:

Somewhere outside Guadalajara, around 2 AM, Carlos suddenly pulled the bus over onto the dark roadside and shut off the engine. He walked down the aisle and shook us awake. "Get off the bus." I blinked at him. "Excuse me?" Carlos grabbed our bags. I grabbed them back. For a few seconds, we had a silent tug-of-war over our belongings.

I looked outside. It was pitch black. No streetlights, no other people—just an old red car parked nearby, trunk open, waiting for something. A few shadowy figures stood near it, speaking quietly.

"Get in the car," Carlos said. Let me just say, even if I spoke Spanish fluently, this would have been terrifying. But in this case, we understood nothing, except that we were being told to get into a random car in the middle of nowhere. I turned to Kata. Her eyes were wide with fear. She later told me she had one thought running through her head: this is how every kidnapping movie starts.

Kidnapped? Or Just Screwed Over?:

Carlos, apparently, was not coming with us. That made everything even worse. A completely new driver, some guy we had never seen before, was now loading our bags into his trunk. I immediately had one thought: If we stop anywhere, even for a second, someone could grab our stuff and vanish.

So, I pointed at the backseat instead. "Put the bags here," I said, trying to sound confident. He hesitated, then threw them into the car. At this point, Carlos gave us a final wave and walked off into the night. We were left standing there, trying to decide: Do we get into this car or not? We didn't have time to debate. Before we could react, we were shoved into the car, and within seconds, we were speeding off into the unknown.

A Night Drive to Nowhere:

For 30 minutes, we drove in complete silence, the only sound was the hum of the engine and our own rapid breathing.

Where were we going? No idea. Then, finally, we saw lights. A bus station. The car stopped. Our driver pointed at a bus. "This one," he said. We grabbed our bags and got on without a word. Apparently, the first bus had dumped us because it wasn't worth driving just two passengers the last 500 kilometers. That should have been obvious, but at 2 AM, after nearly being left on the side of the road, logical thinking wasn't our strong suit.

We sat there, exhausted, watching as drug dealers wandered the station, offering us everything under the sun. We ignored them. At this point, the only thing we wanted was to get to Mexico City and get the hell out of Mexico. That part of the journey was finally over.

But looking back, that insane ride had already given us one important realization: We weren't the same people who had left California. This trip was already changing us. And we weren't even in Peru yet.

Mexico City to Lima – From Chaos to Clean Streets:

One Last Ride with No Surprises (Hopefully) The moment we stepped off the bus in Mexico City, we had one objective: get to the airport as fast as humanly possible. We hailed a taxi straight from the bus terminal, threw our bags in the trunk, and within minutes, we were standing in front of the ticket counter.

The flight to Lima, Peru was scheduled for the next afternoon, with a layover in Costa Rica. But at that moment, we weren't thinking about flights, border crossings, or itineraries.

All we wanted was a long, scalding hot shower and a clean bed. Luckily, there was a motel within walking distance of the airport. We checked in, scrubbed off three days of accumulated filth, put on fresh clothes, and without wasting another second, rushed into the heart of Mexico City—hungry, thirsty, and desperate to remember that life outside a moving bus existed.

Mexico City: An Overstimulating Paradise:

Mexico City was a shock to the senses—in the best possible way. Massive cathedrals, stunning museums, and centuries-old buildings stood proudly next to lively, European-style streets, bursting with movement and color. And the food? Phenomenal.

We devoured grilled chicken with spicy salsa from a busy street vendor, then strolled down 5 de Mayo Street, heading straight for Zócalo—one of the largest squares in the world. After marveling at the Catedral Metropolitana and spotting a statue of Jesus on a cellphone (yes, really), we hopped in a taxi to visit the Museo Nacional de Antropología. This place was huge. The museum had entire sections dedicated to: Teotihuacán, Toltecs, Mexica (Aztecs), Oaxaca, Gulf Coast cultures, Maya civilization, Northern and Western Mexico.

We barely scratched the surface, focusing only on the Maya section, and that alone took over an hour. By the time we left, our feet were aching, but we still had one more stop—

La Condesa, a hip neighborhood full of trendy restaurants, tree-lined promenades, and Art Deco architecture.

We wandered through Parque México, a lush green park with a duck pond and roller-skating track, before setting off on a peaceful evening stroll. And then, the sky turned black.

The Bicycle Taxi Disaster:

Out of nowhere, thunder rumbled, and within seconds, rain was pouring down in buckets. We needed shelter. Fast. Instead of running to a café like normal people, we flagged down the first bicycle taxi we saw, threw ourselves inside, and huddled under its tiny umbrella, which barely covered our knees. Problem solved. Right? Wrong.

Because just when we thought we were safe, fate decided to mess with us. The pedal broke off. Our poor driver was already soaked to the bone, and now his bike was falling apart beneath him. We felt terrible. We offered to get out and walk, but he kept shaking his head, repeating "No problem! No problem!" while sweating through the storm.

For another few agonizing blocks, he pushed on—pedal-less, exhausted, and visibly struggling—before we finally insisted on getting out and paying him the full fare anyway. We walked the rest of the way soaked and laughing, both feeling a little guilty about leaving him behind.

Mexico City:

Worth Every Minute. If you ever visit Mexico City, do yourself a favor: spend at least four days here. For food alone, it's worth it. Tamales (corn dough steamed in husks, with or without fillings). Enchiladas (corn tortillas stuffed with meat, covered in spicy chili sauce and melted cheese). Pozole (a rich, meat-and-vegetable soup best enjoyed in a real restaurant). But the true Mexican street food experience? That's tacos.

Tacos are everywhere, served on every street corner, eaten by everyone, multiple times a day. Choose between: Soft flour tortillas or crispy corn tortillas. Steak, fish, or chicken fillings. Always served with fresh salsa and lettuce. Just be careful with the pickled vegetables—one bite of those spicy carrots or cauliflower, and you might cry involuntarily. Everything we ate was so good, I didn't even care what gave me food poisoning. It was worth it.

Almost every vehicle runs on diesel, filling the city with an unbearable stench. The pollution is so bad that the smog layers physically separate, creating a thick haze over the skyline. Some tourists even get nosebleeds from it. (We only coughed for two weeks straight, so I'd call that a win.)

That said, crime wasn't an issue—at least in the tourist-heavy areas. Police officers stood on almost every corner, and despite what guidebooks warned, we didn't experience pickpocketing or robbery. That doesn't mean you should wave your expensive camera around or wander into sketchy neighborhoods, but in general, we felt safe. And most importantly? We got on a plane—finally leaving Carlos and his death trap of a bus behind.

Lima, Peru: Clean Streets and Cautious Tourists The first thing we noticed upon landing in Lima, Peru? Everything was clean. After days of dust, garbage, and burning diesel fumes, stepping onto Lima's well-kept streets was almost surreal. A taxi took us to Miraflores, the safest and most tourist-friendly district—probably where you'd stay if you ever visit.

Apparently, Peru is experiencing a wave of British immigration, thanks to its affordable oceanfront apartments.

No surprise there—if there's one thing Brits love, it's cheap real estate in warm climates.

Where to Stay in Lima: The Flying Dog Hostel We found a budget-friendly gem: Flying Dog Hostel. For $25 per night, we got: A private room, A bathroom (hot water supply... limited)

Breakfast included. There was even WiFi and a tiny travel desk (a literal table) where you could book bus tickets.

Pro tip: DO NOT try walking to the bus station. Unless you have a death wish, take a cab.

Lima: Not Much to See, But Plenty to Eat. There isn't much sightseeing in Lima.

You can: Walk to the cliffs for an ocean view (featuring a giant shopping mall). Admire the dirty beaches (from a safe distance). Wander the main square, get bored within 30 minutes, and leave. But at night, the city transforms.

Street vendors roll out their red food carts, and the feast begins: Butifarra – Sliced boiled meat in a burger bun, topped with crispy onions, lettuce, and an amazing sauce. Picarones – Pumpkin doughnuts, fried to perfection and drenched in honey. Arroz con leche – Rice pudding, layered with hot blueberry jam. We ate everything, and as expected... the diarrhea continued. Worth it.

Next Stop: A 14-Hour Bus Ride to Arequipa.

Hopefully, no Carlos this time.

The Journey South

May 17, 2008

The adventure 40-hour bus ride designed by someone who clearly hated comfort. Straight from Tijuana to Mexico City—restless legs, questionable smells, and a diet of chips and soda to survive.
Distance: 3,050 km. Altitude: 2,240 m (Mexico City). Weather: 25°C and dry.
From Mexico City, we flew through Costa Rica to Lima, Peru—a momentary reprieve from buses before diving deeper into the journey.

May 20, 2008 – Lima, Peru
Lima greeted us with chaos: honking horns, street vendors, and the ever-present fog of diesel fumes. We checked into the Flying Dog Hostel (25 USD/night), where breakfast came with tales of wanderlust from fellow travelers.
Population: 8.8 million. Altitude: 154 m. Weather: 21°C, overcast.
Overnight stay: 1 night.

May 21, 2008 – Lima to Arequipa
We boarded an overnight bus to Arequipa, reclining seats offering little respite. The 1,000-km journey through the Andes was breathtaking but sleepless.
Population: 1.2 million. Altitude: 2,335 m. Weather: 10°C on arrival.
Overnight stay: 1 night on the bus.

May 22, 2008 – Arequipa to Cabanaconde
The journey became more rugged as we moved deeper into the Andes. Dusty roads, dizzying altitudes, and a chicken

riding shotgun marked the bus rides:
- Arequipa to Chivay: 4 hours. Altitude: 3,635 m.
- Chivay to Cabanaconde: 2 hours. Altitude: 3,287 m.

In Cabanaconde, dinner was alpaca stew—unfortunately followed by food poisoning. The room? A cold-water shower and a dirty mattress fit for nightmares.
Population: 3,300. Weather: 15°C, clear.
Overnight stay: 1 night.

May 23, 2008 – Cabanaconde to Arequipa
Leaving Cabanaconde, we bumped along treacherous roads back to Arequipa.
Distance: 180 km. Weather: 16°C, dry. Altitude: 2,335 m.

May 24, 2008 – Arequipa to Cuzco
A grueling 13-hour bus ride took us to Cuzco, the heart of the Inca Empire. Altitude sickness hit hard, but the charm of cobblestones and ruins kept us going.
Population: 435,000. Altitude: 3,399m. Weather: 14°C, sunny.

May 27, 2008 – Cuzco to Machu Picchu
We set out pre-dawn to Ollantaytambo, followed by a scenic train ride to Aguas Calientes. By noon, we stood before the majestic Machu Picchu, its misty allure leaving us speechless.
Distance from Cuzco: 70 km. Altitude: 2,430 m (Machu Picchu). Weather: 20°C, misty.
Overnight stay: 1 night in Cuzco.

June 1, 2008 – Santiago, Chile
Crossing borders, we arrived in Santiago.
Population: 5.6 million. Altitude: 520 m. Weather: 18°C, crisp.

Here, we learned the hard way about travel scams. A "better room" pitch ended with Kata's passport and $400

stolen. Hours at the embassy and frantic paperwork followed.
Overnight stay: 2 nights.

June 5, 2008 – Neuquén, Argentina
A peaceful stop in Neuquén brought relief after endless bus rides. Medialunas (crescent pastries) were a highlight.
Population: 365,000. Altitude: 260 m. Weather: 10°C, cool.
Overnight stay: 1 night.

June 6, 2008 – Buenos Aires, Argentina
Buenos Aires dazzled us with tango, café culture, and vibrant streets.
Population: 13 million. Altitude: 25 m. Weather: 19°C, sunny.
Overnight stay: 5 nights.

June 11, 2008 – Montevideo, Uruguay
A ferry ride took us to Montevideo, Uruguay's laid-back capital. It was a city for sunsets and slow days.
Population: 1.3 million. Altitude: 43 m. Weather: 22°C, breezy.
Overnight stay: 1 night.

June 15, 2008 – Rio de Janeiro, Brazil
By mid-June, we reached Rio's vibrant chaos. Samba beats filled the air as we stayed at the Bamboo Rio Hostel.
Population: 6.7 million. Altitude: 2 m. Weather: 27°C, sunny.
Overnight stay: 5 nights.

June 30, 2008 – The End of the Road
After 43 days, over 7,000 km traveled, 7 countries, 25 overnight stays, and countless memories, we flew home from São Paulo via KLM. The journey was exhausting,

exhilarating, and unforgettable.

The Numbers Behind the Adventure
- Distance Covered: 7,000+ km across 7 countries.
- Highest Altitude: Chivay, Peru – 3,635 m.
- Longest Bus Ride: 40 hours (Los Angeles to Mexico City).
- Overnight Stays: 25 nights in 5 countries.

Weather Extremes:
- Hottest Day: 27°C in Rio de Janeiro.
- Coldest Night: 8°C in Cabanaconde.

Budget Breakdown:
- Bus Costs: ~$200 USD.
- Accommodations: ~$500 USD.

Food & Culture:
- Meals Sampled: 40+, including alpaca stew, medialunas, tamales, and feijoada.
- Wildlife Encounters: Condors in Colca Canyon, llamas in Machu Picchu, monkeys at Iguazú Falls.

Highlights:
- Most Breathtaking View: Sunrise over Machu Picchu.
- Most Memorable Incident: Passport stolen in Chile, requiring a frantic embassy trip.

Death Road of the Andes, The Cabanaconde to Arequipa Bus Ride:

The road from Cabanaconde to Arequipa isn't just a bus ride. It's an endurance test, a gamble with physics, and a masterclass in high-altitude suffering. If there were ever a road that made you question your mortality while simultaneously offering the most breathtaking views of your life, this would be it.

The Route: Numbers That Make You Sweat
- Distance: 200 km (124 miles)
- Duration: 5-6 hours (or eternity, depending on road conditions and driver enthusiasm)
- Highest Point: Patapampa Pass – 4,910 meters (16,109 feet)
- Starting Altitude: Cabanaconde – 3,287 meters (10,784 feet)
- Ending Altitude: Arequipa – 2,335 meters (7,661 feet)
- Key Villages Passed: Chivay, Maca, Yanque

This road takes you from the thin, frigid air of the high Andes down to the relatively mild climate of Arequipa. In between, it delivers hairpin turns, gut-wrenching cliff edges, and enough elevation changes to leave your lungs gasping for oxygen.

The Road Itself: A Masterpiece of Madness
Paved? Yes. Safe? Not even close. The road snakes its way through one of the world's deepest canyons, where every curve is a new opportunity for disaster. Landslides are common. Blind corners? Plenty. Guardrails? Minimal, because apparently, that would ruin the thrill.

Buses frequently overtake slower vehicles on curves with zero visibility, while steep switchbacks require the driver to swing into oncoming traffic just to make the turn. If the altitude doesn't get you, the adrenaline will.

Altitude & Weather, Your Body vs. The Andes:
- At Cabanaconde, the air is already thin, but by the time you hit Patapampa Pass at 4,910 meters (16,109 feet), you're in hypoxia territory.
- Oxygen levels: 40% lower than at sea level.
- Temperatures: Drop below freezing at night, with

howling winds making it feel even worse.
- Arequipa: By the time you descend to 2,335 meters (7,661 feet), it feels like you've been reborn into a land of warmth and oxygen.

Scenery, Beautiful Enough to Distract You from Death:
It's not all terror—there's also sheer, mind-blowing beauty.
- Colca Canyon: Twice as deep as the Grand Canyon. The road clings to its edges like it wasn't designed to support human life.
- Volcanoes: Misti, Chachani, and Ampato stand like ancient gods, watching your foolish attempt at survival.
- Wildlife: Andean condors soar overhead, perhaps already scouting potential carcasses. Vicuñas and llamas graze on the high-altitude plains, oblivious to your suffering.

Danger & Fatalitie, The Dark Side of the View:
- Accidents: Bus crashes are not uncommon, especially during the rainy season when landslides turn the road into a death trap.
- Fatalities: Exact numbers are elusive, but between reckless drivers, unpaved detours, and the lack of oxygen, it's one of Peru's riskiest routes.
- Motion Sickness: If the altitude doesn't get you, the endless switchbacks will. Vomiting is almost a rite of passage.

The Ride Itself, A Case Study in Fear:

The driver, unfazed by the apocalypse outside the windshield, speeds along like he's late for his own funeral. Coca-chewing locals remain disturbingly calm, while wide-eyed tourists grip their seats, silently making peace with their gods.

The turns are so tight that the bus swings wildly, sometimes requiring a three-point maneuver just to complete a curve. The only thing standing between you and the abyss? A flimsy metal railing, if you're lucky.

After hours of near-death experiences, the road flattens. The altitude drops. Oxygen returns. Arequipa appears like a mirage.

You stagger off the bus, delirious, grateful, and vowing never to do that again.

Would I recommend it? Absolutely. Once.

The Last Wait

Szántód, Hungary 2008

The family house, by Lake Balaton. The old inn—The Black Bridge—now just a skeleton of its past, held together by bad plumbing and the smell of stale beer.

The grill still stood near the terrace—lava stones buried in dust, its iron grates streaked with the blackened crust of old schnitzels and one last pot of chili con carne.

Inside, the walls had yellowed from decades of cigarette smoke. Every chair, every drawer, every doorframe reeked of ash and warm beer. That permanent stink of old bars.

Downstairs: the kocsma, barely breathing, where my father tried and failed to resurrect the old magic as a drinkery for the lonely and the lost.

Upstairs: my grandmother, dying in slow motion. But not dying fast enough. Let's not pretend it was peaceful.

It was ugly.

Her body shrank, skin clinging to bones like wet paper. She stank. Of sickness. Of rotting flesh. Of something spiritual.

And worse than the smell? The sound.

She didn't cry. She moaned. Day and night. A long, eerie groan that came from somewhere deeper than pain. Not just physical — existential. People at the bar below could hear it.

Imagine sipping your fröccs while something upstairs howls like a banshee trapped in purgatory.

And here's the twist: I don't think God let her go because she didn't deserve a clean exit.

This was the same woman who—and I swear I felt this growing up—helped her husband die.

No one ever said it. But we knew. Grandpa didn't have cancer. No real illness. He just… stopped. Like someone put a pillow on his face one night and ended it.

And who would've done that? The same woman who yelled at him for seventy years, beating him without reason. The same woman who couldn't stand his breathing.

She cooked his food for eighty years and probably decided when his time was up.

Maybe this was justice. God's payback.

She couldn't walk. Couldn't eat. Couldn't die.

She just oozed misery into the house. For months.

While we were backpacking in South America—eating street food, getting lost, living like the young idiots we were—she was up there rotting in her own skin.

When we got home, my father barely looked me in the eye. "She's upstairs," he said.

I stood at the bottom of the stairs.

The smell and sound followed me. Moaning. Faint, wet, like she was dissolving slowly in acid.

I didn't go up. I couldn't.

Kata did.

She climbed the creaking stairs. Grandma stirred.

"Who's here?" she asked, voice thin, brittle. "Laszlo came home," Kata said.

She smiled—barely. That twisted, bone-thin face stretched into something like a grin.

And then... she died. Just like that. Five minutes after I got home.

She waited. Not for my father. Not for peace.

For me.

To know I was safe. Back from the world. To hear it with her own ears—Laszlo came home.

Then she could finally clock out. I didn't even say goodbye. Maybe she didn't need me to. Just knowing I was back was enough.

Enough to end the war she'd been fighting alone.

A Dream on the Rocks – Malta

The Man by the Harbor

It's early morning in Marsaskala, and the harbor is waking up. The old men drag out their domino tables, grumbling their way into the day. Fishermen sort their nets with half a cigarette dangling from their lips, the occasional slap of a fish against the deck breaking the silence. In the overpriced rentals along the promenade, tourists snore through the sunrise, unaware of the world they paid to visit.

Down by the narrow streets, someone moves fast. Too fast for the heat, too fast for his age. A wiry frame, wrapped in sun-bleached clothes, dodging through the waking town with a sense of urgency that doesn't seem to match anything around him.

Every morning, the same path. Past the quiet German restaurant, the one with white tablecloths but no customers, a place that looks more like a money-laundering front than a business. Past the limestone ruins, where stray cats stretch in the shade, blinking at the world like they've seen it all and weren't impressed.

At the edge of the rocks, he crouches. Bare hands scrape the shore, gathering sea salt, rubbing it between fingers, dropping it into thick canvas sacks. A process slow and methodical, like a man harvesting his own survival. Salt is never bought. Why would it be? It's right there.

Behind him, the cats watch. A shifting army of forty, maybe sixty, some limping, some sleek, all waiting. He complains about them, of course. Too many. Always hungry. The council should do something. But at sunset, bowls appear. The complaints continue, but the feeding never stops.

Inside the tall, narrow house, letters pile up. Pages and pages of meticulous handwriting—complaints to the council, reports on street conditions, noise violations, unauthorized boats in the harbor. A ledger of grievances, a map of minor injustices. When the last envelope is sealed, the binoculars come out. From the tiny window, a full view of the harbor. The domino players, the fishermen, the lost tourists. The coming and going of ships. Nothing escapes the gaze. The harbor never stops moving. And neither does he. His name is John. And somehow, he became our friend.

Malta Was Hot, Dry, and Covered in Limestone Dust

We came to Marsaskala with a plan and just enough money to believe in it. A restaurant—small, simple, honest. We found the spot rotting next to a greasy fried chicken takeaway. The walls were stained with fryer oil, the electrical wiring looked like a fire waiting to happen, and the floors were so saturated with grease that they fought back when we tried to rip them up. We signed a 30-year lease like lunatics. Then we tore it apart.

The harbor still had its charm—luzzus rocking on the tide, painted up in fever-dream blues and yellows, nets slung over docks like abandoned hopes.

But the streets? A greasy smear of fried chicken takeaways and sunburned Brits in cargo shorts, tripping over their own drunken bravado.

Somewhere in that mess, hunched between a biohazard takeaway and a crumbling limestone relic, was the husk that would become Tal Latini, a restaurant built from ruins. "Restaurant" was generous. It was a corpse. The walls held the echo of menus that never made it past Tuesday. But we had a lease, a half-mad vision, and nothing to lose.

John Vella – The Man Who Owned Malta's Secrets

We met John Vella through Derril, an old American-Hungarian friend of Kata's. Vella wasn't just a real estate agent—he was a walking archive of Malta's underbelly. Which flats had the best views, who was late on rent, where you could get your hands on something "off the books."

He knew everyone and everything.

Need a deal? A workaround? A favor that might technically be illegal? Vella had a guy.

Now he was our guy. Our go-to guy for anything that came with a wink and no paperwork.

Demolition, Malta-Style:

First step: Burn the past. Anything that wasn't nailed down, we tore out. Then we realized most of it was nailed down, so we tore that out too. Vella, always full of bright ideas and questionable execution, showed up with his underpowered, wheezing moped —a relic that looked like it had survived a small war and lost. The thing rattled like a shopping cart with a grudge and belched blue smoke every time he touched the throttle. It was barely strong enough to carry one man and a loaf of bread, let alone two grown men and a stack of rotting timber. But in Vella's mind, it was the perfect solution. Cheaper than a van, faster than walking, and—according to him—"still technically road legal."

Imagine it: two grown men bouncing over Marsaskala's cracked, medieval roads, hauling salvaged doors and busted wooden beams, the moped coughing like a smoker on his last pack. Every pothole was a death trap. Every turn kicked up a dust cloud that tasted like divorce and diesel. Oncoming cars honked around blind corners out of habit—not caution—whether anyone was there or not. Horse-drawn carriages clopped by like we'd time-traveled to the 1800s. Behind us, a procession of stray cats trailed the other John—the British one—like he was their personal messiah.

We scavenged like pirates with bad planning.

- An old wooden boat mast, dragged from a dockyard graveyard.

- A pile of discarded glass bottles, reborn as glass bricks for the dark corner of bathroom walls.

- Doorframes that had seen more history than some small countries.

Tal Latini wasn't getting built—it was being resurrected.

The Look of a Place That Had Always Been There:

If we were going to do this, it couldn't feel new. Tal Latini had to look like it had grown out of the island, like it had been there before electricity, before tourists, before Malta even had a name. We wanted salt in the walls, sunburn in the wood, a place that smelled like sea spray and old stories.

Kata scavenged forgotten window frames, sanding and painting them until they looked like they'd been ripped from a shipwreck and kissed by time. The front door? Built by a local boatwright — a man whose hands were all bone and rope, whose patience had been shaped by a lifetime of saltwater and storms.

Walls weren't just painted—they were textured, beaten, made to look like they'd held up against storms and time. Tables? Thick, raw slabs of wood. Chairs? Built strong in

Italy to survive a brawl. Lighting? Lanterns, flickering like the belly of an old ship.

Even the salt on the tables—British John's brilliant madness—came from the very shore where he scraped it up every morning, stuffing it into canvas sacks like buried treasure.

There were no blueprints. No corporate aesthetic. Tal Latini wasn't designed. It was found.

The Kitchen:

Of course, no restoration story is complete without a bit of stupidity. Ours came in the form of a second-hand, professional-grade kitchen that had no business being inside that building.

The oven didn't fit through the door. The ventilation was a fire hazard waiting to be interviewed on the evening news. The walk-in fridge only made it in after we took a wall out—and part of our dignity with it. The grease trap met EU regulations on paper. That was the best we could say.

We pieced the whole thing together like war scavengers, hitting up abandoned kitchens across Valletta. Real end-of-the-line stuff—stainless steel counters pitted with burn marks, fridge units that still hummed like they were holding a grudge. Vella was the mouthpiece. He'd talk a dying man out of his shoes, and walk away claiming he'd done the guy a favor. And honestly? He probably had.

And then we lit the fires. The food? As raw as the place itself. I aged the ribeye wrapped in cheesecloth—21 days until the funk turned sharp and nutty. Cut to order, sold by weight. Some came thick as a butcher's forearm. Others small, fast, and gone in three bites. Seafood so fresh and salads that didn't fuck around with kale or quinoa. No frills. No nonsense. Just real food tasted like someone gave a damn. And for one golden summer, it worked.

The Other John – Prophet of Nothing

While we were sanding, hammering, sweating to bring Tal Latini to life, the other John—the British one—sat outside, peering through his binoculars like he was watching a slow-motion shipwreck.

Every day. Not to eat. Not to help. Just to sit, sip coffee, and spin stories about the millions he was "about to make" in Forex.

"Demo's easy, mate," he'd say, casual as a weather report. "Real money? That's when you lose your nerve—and your shirt."

I'd be at the grill, dodging sparks, elbows deep in steaks and lamb chops, and there he was—posted up like a pub philosopher, diagnosing the end of the financial world without lifting a finger.

At the time, I thought he was just lonely and bored. Looking back? Maybe he was the only one who saw what was coming. Something real.

Restaurants pop up like mushrooms and vanish just as fast. We knew the odds. But Tal Latini wasn't just another name on a weathered signboard. It was scraped knuckles, makeshift repairs, sea breeze in your bones. A busted moped, a stolen boat mast. Stray cats acting like landlords. Then our priorities changed. Kata was pregnant. We had €2,000 to our name. The numbers didn't lie: we weren't going to turn a profit that first season — maybe not even the next. So we shut the door, flew home to have the baby, and promised ourselves we'd come back next summer. Spoiler: we didn't.

No big meltdown. No cinematic ending. Just life moving forward — fast.

Smoke, Bees, and Burnt Wood

The mornings started before the sun had a chance to think. Fog clung low over the frozen fields of Karád, a sleepy Hungarian village where even time seemed to move slower. The only real motion was smoke curling into the pale sky—and Sándor bácsi, already up, already working, already swearing.

Sándor wasn't a man. He was an element. Somewhere between firewood and iron. Seventy-something, built like an ox that survived a war, with fists like knotted roots and a work ethic that would put a diesel engine to shame. He didn't talk much unless it was to insult modern tools or complain about the softness infecting the younger generation.

And he had bees. Lots of them.

Dozens of hives lined the edge of his orchard like weathered filing cabinets humming with fury. He never wore a mask, never gloves—just walked among them like some pagan beekeeper god, lifting the lids, checking frames, tapping and scraping with bare, cracked hands while bees swarmed his face like it was just Tuesday. He'd mutter things to them—short words in his deep voice, as if negotiating peace or reminding them who built the place.

I once asked him why he didn't wear protection.

He just shrugged. "If you're calm, they're calm. They feel fear. Like dogs. Or wives."

Whatever he was doing, it worked. His honey was thick, golden, alive. The kind you could smell through the jar. He sold it by the barrel to German buyers who drove down in shiny black vans with no plates and left with half a ton of Hungarian sunlight in liquid form. Sándor didn't bother bottling it or marketing it. You wanted labels, you went to the supermarket. You wanted honey that could cure your cold and maybe resurrect your grandfather, you came to Sándor.

"We burn it black," he grunted, tossing another fence post onto a mountain of logs. "Burn it 'til it turns to armor. Eighty years—nothing touches it. Not bugs. Not water. Not time." And with that, he rolled an old tire onto the pyre and lit it.

The smoke that followed was hellish—thick, black, and sticky. It clung to your lungs and your soul. Flames roared through frozen brush, embers flying like angry spirits. We stood too close, cutting, stacking, lifting logs the size of dead horses while the sweat poured under winter coats. It was below freezing, but we were soaked. We weren't clearing land. We were exorcising it.

Sándor moved like a man possessed—swinging axes, dragging logs. He was strict, like a German general with a heart buried somewhere under fifty years of bark. But he paid daily, in cash, and he fed us from a tin lunchbox that tasted like history. That winter, he gave me more than work. He gave me a way to crawl back. After Tal Latini collapsed and we limped back to Hungary with a baby and an empty wallet, we needed something more than survival. We needed rhythm. Purpose. Routine. Sándor gave me that. One fence post, one log, one smoked lungful at a time.

We lived in Nágocs, at my mother's house. A dead-end village—one road in, none out. No gypsies, no outsiders, no traffic. Just quiet, the wind, and the bell. The church bell rang like a heartbeat, the only thing that moved on purpose.

When it rang, it made the place feel whole—like something ancient had stirred and settled again, it echoed off the hills like God clearing his throat.

They said the bell kept the demons away. And it must've worked—because nothing ever happened in Nágocs. No fires, no visitors, no passionate affairs. Even the cats looked bored. The demons took one look and moved on to somewhere with better nightlife.

Our house walls were thick adobe, packed with hay and the weight of old lives. Inside, it was warm and quiet. The búbos kemence—that great dome of earth and fire—sat in the middle of the room like a sleeping animal, shaped like a barrel, wide enough to sit on, to lean your back against its warmth. You'd load it once before bed, and by morning it still breathed heat into the room. I brought in sawdust-dusted firewood under one arm, through snow and mud—just enough to keep the rhythm. We didn't cook in it, though we could have. My mother dried things on top: lemongrass for tea, walnuts from the giant tree in the garden. Quiet work. Slow heat. Nothing wasted.

That's when Janka, our daughter, gave me my new name. FaFa.

She couldn't say "apa" yet. But every time she saw me hauling logs, she'd smile and shout "FaFa!"—wood wood. It stuck. It broke me in the best way. I was no longer just a failed restaurateur or a struggling chef. I was her FaFa. Her warmth in winter. Her fire bringer.

Kata, stepped into motherhood with a grace that caught me off guard. One minute she was painting walls in Malta, fighting through restaurant collapse, and the next she was holding our daughter with a calm fierceness I'd never seen. She gave Janka light, rhythm, joy—even when money was tight, even when the house creaked with old age and cold drafts. She never complained. She never panicked. She just mothered like she was born to do it.

My mother, for all her sharp tongue and blunt honesty, never said a word. Not one argument in an entire year of us staying in her home. A miracle. She was calm, quiet, observant. She'd mutter the occasional comment about politicians or the neighbor's rooster, but when it came to us—nothing. Just silent support. A woman who knew how to grow tomatoes in clay and survive on scraps didn't need to lecture. She let us do what we had to. She gave us space, warmth, and her strange, miraculous garden.

Her garden was alive with contradiction. Citrus trees near pines, mint woven into marjoram, onions beside roses. A labyrinth of chaos that somehow bloomed every season. She threw nothing away. The garbage bin sat untouched for weeks. Everything was reused, replanted, composted, transformed. The woman could feed a village from a plot the size of a living room.

Evenings were slow. Janka asleep, curled like a cat under wool blankets. Milka, the dog, snoring by the oven, twitching in her sleep. We sat at the kitchen table talking about the future in low voices like it might hear us and run away.

Despite having almost no money, we never skipped baby swimming. Kaposvár was a journey, but we made it. We'd drive with the engine off down every hill, rolling silent, clutching the wheel like smugglers dodging fuel costs. Every forint mattered—but seeing her in that blue water, tiny arms waving, eyes wide with wonder? That was wealth. When summer came, the heat didn't slow us. Sándor's fires still raged, his chainsaw still screamed, and we worked like it was wartime. I still carried wood under my arm. Still FaFa.

Sometimes we'd splurge on a trip to the thermal baths in Igal. Soaking in hot, mineral-rich water while old villagers gossiped and soaked like lazy hippos—it was a different kind of therapy. A reminder that life didn't have to hurt every second.

Money came in slow trickles, like sap from a tired tree. But the stress was gone. We ate from the garden. We repaired what we broke. And every day, I watched my daughter unfold—her laugh, her clumsy steps, her curiosity. It was messy, imperfect magic.

The village had its characters. The kocsma was center stage. Half the men were philosophers, the other half professional drinkers. Cigarettes permanently glued to their lips, they leaned on the bar like it was holding up the world. Homemade wine in plastic soda bottles. Pálinka that could knock out a mule. And jokes—God, the jokes. Dirty, ancient, hilarious.

One guy claimed he once won a goat in a poker game and lost it five minutes later betting on a chicken race. Someone else swore he'd met Sean Connery in Balatonfüred. Maybe he had. Who knows? In villages like these, truth was optional, but the storytelling was mandatory.

In California, I'd cooked for millionaires. Smoked salmon towers, avocado air, all that tweezer-food bullshit. Now I was boiling potatoes and chopping onions, and no one needed a menu. Just food. We had heat. We had food. We had a baby who called me FaFa and thought I hung the moon because I could light a fire.

After everything we lost, we'd somehow found something better. Harmony.

Not perfect. Not easy. But real. And that made all the difference.

After a year, we moved to Budapest—closer to Kata's mother in Pasarét. We found a modest one-bedroom flat: old parquet floors, a wheezing radiator, and just enough space to live without stepping on each other. It wasn't much, but it felt like a fresh start. I was ready to go back to the line.

Word on the street was that river cruise ships paid well—especially for cooks who could handle pressure without crying or quitting. Long hours, high standards, good money. I'd cooked for millionaires in California. I figured I could handle a few spoiled tourists floating down the Danube.

So I shaved, updated my CV, and went looking for a uniform that still fit.

Back to the Steel Beast

Three years on a river cruise ship. That's how I paid for diapers, rent, and the illusion that I was still in control. I traded the soft Hungarian earth for stainless steel floors that never stopped vibrating. The galley became my world—claustrophobic, thrumming, relentless. They called it fine dining. I called it an endurance test with no finish line—limitless, unforgiving, and just sane enough to keep going.

The ship looked glamorous in the brochures—golden sunsets on the Danube, sun hats and Riesling, swans drifting past baroque cathedrals. White linen on the sundeck. Bottled charm and fake smiles. It promised elegance, refinement, and riverfront serenity.

In reality, we sailed a fixed route: two-week round trips between Budapest and Amsterdam, nonstop from March to November. Occasionally a Cologne-based detour or a chartered cruise through the northern German rivers, but mostly it was that same stretch—up the Rhine, down the Danube, repeat. A luxury loop for guests. A pressure loop for us in a galley that pulsed with fluorescent lights, tension, and the unholy blend of fryer oil, recycled air, and burnout. Every shift was a ten-hour sprint. Small windows, the hum of compressors, the clatter of knives, and muttered curses in ten languages. Some guys never slept. Some didn't speak. One guy got caught cooking shirtless with a cigarette tucked under his chef hat. Another, a dishwasher from Romania sharpened his knife on the prep table edge like he was back in prison. Drunk.

We worked like animals, fought like brothers, and laughed like lunatics. The food was good, sometimes great. But it didn't matter. You learn things on a ship. How to function on no sleep. How to scream without moving your face. How to cook while sliding in grease. You learn what adrenaline mixed with instant coffee feels like. You learn that fear has a smell, and it doesn't mix with béchamel. You learn that your limits aren't where you thought they were. They're much further out. And uglier. You don't rise to the occasion—you sink into it. You stretch. You break. You keep going. Because there's no other choice. The guests want dinner. The ship keeps moving. And somewhere in that motion, you discover something terrifying and liberating: you can take more than you ever imagined.

But I made money. I called Kata every night, voice cracking over satellite lines. Janka would scream into the receiver, calling for FaFa. I missed bedtime stories. Baby swimming. Her first teeth. Her first real words—beyond "wood wood." It killed me. But I kept going. Because the ship didn't stop.

We weren't feeding tourists. We were staging a luxury opera for people who couldn't hear anymore. The ingredients? Unreal. Tauck cruises spared no expense. Black Angus tenderloins smuggled into Europe like high-end narcotics. Racks of New Zealand lamb packed tighter than our egos. Foie Gras, wild berries, custom-spiced veal demi-glace—all for customers who'd rather have well-done steak and complain about the water pressure.

Now picture this: a river cruise ship slicing through the Rhine like a hot knife through warm strudel. Below deck, the galley—tight as a sprung coffin trap—felt like a locked shipping container in the eye of a storm, walls closing in. The cooks? Mainly Filipino, mostly polite, humble, quiet—but absolute machines. Unstoppable. Unshakeable. Repeating the same motions every day like they were born on a conveyor belt.

Some of them didn't even know where they were. Plucked from rice fields in Lombok or Jakarta, flown in through shady agencies that promised paradise and delivered Bamberg. No maps. No choices. Just contracts and orders. One of them told me about The Flood—a real one. Lost his house. His dog. Spent two months barefoot in a school gym. Another lost 20 kilos during Ramadan. I thought he had cancer. "No, sir," he said, smiling. "Discipline." And when I gave them their first sip of my village pálinka—70% proof, raw Hungarian rocket fuel—they lost their minds. "Sir... this is medicine." "No," I grinned. "This is freedom."

If you survived the first two weeks without blood, tears, or a full mental collapse—you were already management material. Breakfast buffet. Lunch service. Afternoon snacks. Dinner à la carte. Midnight cleanup. Repeat. Eight months straight.

After week three, your soul checks out. It just quietly packs a bag and slips out the service exit without saying goodbye. You don't even notice until you try to laugh at a joke and realize your mouth forgot how.

By week six, time stops making sense. Days blur together into one long loop of eggs Benedict and floor sanitizer. Monday becomes Thursday becomes God-knows-what-day-it-is. You stop counting hours and start counting prep lists. The only calendar is the delivery schedule. The only way out? When the river swells too high or drops dangerously low, we grind to a halt. Sometimes stranded in the middle of nowhere. Sometimes stuck for a week—or until the damn river lets us move again.

By week ten, you're not even a person anymore. You're just hands and reflexes—muscle memory soaked in sweat and burned out adrenaline. You move like a haunted marionette: chopping, flipping, yelling at shadows. You catch yourself saying "behind" to your wife on the phone. You dream about food labels. You start referring to home as "shore leave." You could be on fire and still finish plating the risotto before asking for burn cream. And the worst part? You start to like it.

We had Amsterdam, it was always the restart button. End of one cruise, beginning of another. The guests changed, the menus reset, and we braced ourselves for another two-week descent down the Rhine. But the best part? Those two wild nights between disembarkation and the fresh batch of luxury zombies.

First night: the old guests were still onboard, clinking wine glasses and pretending they weren't hungover from fourteen straight days of "cultural immersion." They looked exhausted. Shell-shocked. Dragged across half of Europe like rich livestock—force-fed history, wine, and medieval architecture. Too many vineyards. Too many churches. Too many goddamn cobblestones. They couldn't tell Vienna from Würzburg anymore. You'd hear them mumble, "Another cathedral?" like someone had just insulted their mother. Second day: cleaning everything—from fryer filters to crew souls. Third night: new passengers embarked—wide-eyed, wrinkle-faced, and freshly dry-cleaned. Ready for the river dream.

They smiled like they were stepping into a fairy tale. No clue they were walking into a slow-motion blender of early wake-up calls, lukewarm folklore, and back-to-back excursions narrated by the same bored guide. Twelve days of wine, history, and polite clapping—until their brains turned to soft cheese and every baroque church blurred into one holy migraine. They weren't guests. They were tribute to the gods of mass tourism, sacrifices to the itinerary. Forced enthusiasm, hearing the phrase "this village was first mentioned in 1247" at least a dozen times. But in between all that? Two nights of semi-freedom. And Amsterdam doesn't waste your time. That night, we wandered the red glow alleys and crooked canal bridges like escaped prisoners on shore leave. Someone handed us a plastic bag with a cookie inside. "Space cookie," they said. "Start with half. Takes about an hour."

Naturally, we ignored every word of advice. "It's probably bullshit," Diego laughed, already halfway through his. Whispered, "Sir… this is crazy."

"No," I said. "This is survival."

I ate the whole thing because I didn't want to carry it.

An hour later, we were absolutely unhinged. Not high in the usual sense. This was astral projection in chef shoes. Like that little hypnotic helix usually sold as a wind spinner, often tagged "spiral wind spinner," "twister," or, in old-school lingo, a whirligig. It hangs by a swivel hook so the whole spiral glints and corkscrews whenever a breeze rolls past—pretty much the exact kaleidoscope effect you got from that Amsterdam space-cookie trip.

That was Amsterdam.

Of course, the river waits for no idiot. Next night, we sailed—new passengers on board, new white coats, same old descent into culinary madness.

I wasn't just the sous chef—I was Executive Chef now, already. A tight soldier, second in command after the captain himself. The uniform had weight, but the real authority came from the burns on your arms and the bags under your eyes. You didn't lead with your mouth. You led with your scars.

Every second week had one word hanging over it like a curse: Loading.
It meant we'd dock somewhere near Passau, meet four massive lorries at some forgotten industrial road, and have exactly thirty minutes—no more—to load every single thing the ship needed for the next two weeks. Food for 200 guests, 40 crew, drinks, chemicals, napkins, wine, vegetables, meat, eggs. Thousands of eggs.

All crew member lined up—bar staff, waiters, receptionists, even the hairdresser if we had one. Nobody was exempt. It was a human conveyor belt, sweating through humid days, cursed rain, or evil, brain-melting heat—dodging collapsing boxes and slipping on plastic wrap. At the end of the chain? Us. The kitchen crew. Eleven to thirteen maniacs, shoulder to shoulder, ready to catch whatever came flying our way.

And I mean flying. We didn't hand things off gently. Hell no. We launched boxes down the chain. Frozen chicken to the chest. A sack of onions straight to the gut. We made it a sport. If you missed a box? Too bad. That's dinner sinking into the Danube. At the final end stood the smarter ones, the veterans. Putting things away before the avalanche buried us. Freezer goods came last—bags of peas, beef tenderloins, ice cream tubs—and we shoved it in like Tetris until the door couldn't close. You want something tomorrow? Bring a headlamp and good luck. That freezer was a black hole.

But the real madness hit the night before loading. We called it "making room." That meant one thing: dump everything. Because head office calculated every gram of food for a two-week cruise. If anything was left by the end, it meant we'd screwed up—served too little, portioned too tight, or guests skipped meal. It didn't matter. There was no room for leftovers. Not physically. Not logistically.

So we tossed it. All of it. Perfectly good produce, anything opened, anything soft. Meat. Vegetables. Milk. Cheese. Fish. Into the river. One by one. No ceremony. No debate. Spices stayed. Salt, flour, sugar, dry goods—we kept what we could. Everything else went overboard. Quietly. Efficiently. With just enough shame to remind you you're still human.

We stacked crates by the back door and walked away. That was nightwatch's job. He knew the drill. Don't ask, just throw.

And the bottles? Not just wine—vodka, gin, rum, champagne, limoncello, the half-sipped fantasies of the upper deck—hundreds of them, every night, tossed straight into the river. No sorting. No recycling. Just straight into the black water, like it had always been that way.

The kitchen goes dark. The engine hum fades into low static. Then—clink. splash. clink. splash. At some point, we stopped reacting. You'd walk by the open hatch and see five cases of empty liquor bottles disappear into the current like they never existed. After feeding them all, the kitchen fell silent. I'd step out onto the upper deck—just to breathe. The river lay flat and black, reflecting the stars like shattered diamonds. On both sides, the world sloped up in shadow—vineyards, medieval towers, quiet villages tucked into the hills like sleeping animals. You could smell pine. Hear the distant bark of a dog. And sometimes, just before midnight, a church bell from some forgotten village would echo across the water—soft, hollow, like a reminder.

Just stunning. Surreal. Like floating through a postcard.

And there I was—standing on a five-star buffet boat, dumping garbage into one of Europe's great arteries. And I'd think: what the fuck are we doing?

There's something undeniably funny about chefs drinking in secret. I don't mean a cheeky pint after service—I'm talking covert ops. Kitchen espionage. Walk-in warfare.

I saw it in their eyes: glazed over, mechanical, like workers trapped in a dish pit purgatory. They chopped. They plated. They wiped down stainless steel with religious discipline. But underneath that silence was exhaustion. Deep, bone-level burnout that no double espresso could fix.

So one night, after feeding 200 Australians like it was nothing, I snapped off my gloves and muttered:

"Walk-in. Now." They froze. Looked at each other. Thought I was joking. You don't break protocol on a river ship. You don't even breathe wrong. But I flashed them the sign—two fingers, like a field commander—and they followed.

We slipped into the walk-in fridge like a team of culinary insurgents. That blast of cold air? Heaven. Behind the frozen spinach, I pulled the contraband: a half-dead bottle of vodka we'd smuggled inside a flour bag. Pulled out plastic ramekins—our communion cups. Silent toast. No words. Just that first freezing shot that lit a fire in our guts.

It wasn't rebellion.
It wasn't tradition.
It was just another way to break the loop that was slowly killing us.

Andre, our pastry guy, blinked and said, "This is how people go missing."

I laughed. "Better to disappear for five minutes than go insane for twelve hours."

From then on, it became ritual. Not every night—just on those perfect nights when service was spotless, prep was done, and all that was left was time, resentment, and a walk-in full of silence. Five minutes of stolen clarity. Then back to the line.

No one ever knew.

We kept our coats white, our boards clean, our timing surgical. One time, the cruise director called us "the most professional team I've ever seen." I nearly choked on my second shot.

That's the thing—no one suspects the kitchen. We're expected to be sweaty, stressed, and screaming into the void. So when we're calm—too calm—they just call it "military precision."

They have no idea.

And this one—this chapter—is for them. For the Filipino boys in the kitchen. They brought lime wedges next time.

Back in chef school, our instructor—a walking cigarette with a moustache—used to send us out for groceries before cooking class. Eggs, onions, flour... and a bottle of Hubertus. Always Hubertus. A bitter Hungarian stomach liquor that tasted like medicinal steeped in radiator fluid. He'd pour himself a shot before demo, then another after yelling at someone for burning a roux. Said it helped him focus. Made him more creative. Honestly? He was sharper and funnier with a buzz.

So yeah—by the time I hit the river, the idea of drinking on the job didn't shock me.

The real shock was how much we needed it just to stay human.

The Ship Eats Its Own

It started with a body on the lobby floor.

Just a pair of feet—pointed outward like a cartoon corpse. One sock halfway off, one shoe dangling like it had given up mid-stride. From behind the lobby bar's fake marble planter, all you could see were those sad, pale ankles and a scattering of sliced cucumber from someone's abandoned spa water.

I slowed down.

Dead?

Could be. It had happened before. Eighty-year-old Americans on their fifth schnapps tour and sixth bypass. One guy choked on a grape during the Captain's Gala. Another slipped in his cabin and died with a sandwich in each hand. Death on river cruises wasn't unheard of. But out in the open, sprawled like a roadkill yoga pose? That was new.

I edged closer. The body wasn't moving. Arms spread wide. Mouth open. Eyes closed, but not peacefully. No dignity. Just theatrical collapse—like a man who wanted to die, but also wanted witnesses.

Then I saw the face.

Paco.

Our sauté guy. Spanish. Part-time philosopher, full-time bullshitter. The undisputed king of kitchen sick days.

"Oh no," I muttered. "Not today."

The receptionist hovered nearby, whispering into her phone like she was ordering an assassination. The hotel manager stood frozen, clutching his tablet like a crucifix. He was sweating through his polyester blazer. "Keep the guests back," he hissed at no one in particular.

Too late.

A Tauck couple was already coming around the corner. Matching beige outfits. Matching stunned expressions. Probably just wanted to ask where the walking tour of Koblenz starts.

"Is he…?" the wife began, hand clutching her cruise lanyard like a rosary.

I jumped in.

"Slip," I said. "Wet floor. Just resting. He's… Spanish."

The husband squinted. "Is that a wine cork in his hand?"

Indeed it was.

Paco had collapsed mid-setup for dinner service, still holding a corkscrew and a bottle opener, like a martyr of hospitality. For a terrifying moment, he truly looked dead. A sunken face, waxy skin, arms flung out in Christ pose on the lobby's fake Persian rug.

The doctor arrived, finally—Dr. Hellmuth, our ship's own slice of Austrian post-apocalyptic medicine. Tall, sunburnt, suspiciously tan for a man who never left the infirmary.

He looked down at Paco the way a butcher looks at a turkey that's faking it.

"Move," he barked.

He knelt beside the body, poked Paco in the ribs like he was testing melon firmness, then tapped his temple twice with a knuckle.

Nothing.

Then—

A moan. Long, drawn-out. Like a hungover whale.

"Heart attack?" someone whispered.

"Stroke?" someone else added.

"Just wants a day off," I muttered.

Hellmuth stood, wiped his hands on a napkin from his pocket, and announced flatly: "Hydration problem. Maybe nerves. Or gas. Not dead."

The manager exhaled like he'd been holding his breath since Vienna.

We dragged Paco's limp body out of the lobby through the crew passage, trying not to leave skid marks on the polished floor. I grabbed his feet, the dishwasher got his shoulders. He smelled like onions. A Romanian steward tossed a blanket over him as we passed a group of curious guests who'd gathered by the bar, snapping photos of the Danube through the window, blissfully unaware.

That was the rule: no dead bodies in the public areas. Bad for business. And Paco, though not technically dead, was definitely not helping sales.

We dumped him on his bunk. He grunted once, rolled over, and pulled his blanket over his head like a teenager dodging chores.

By dinner, he was back in the galley—sweating, silent, eyes hollow. His escape plan crushed under orthopedic shoes and corporate protocol.

Paco didn't speak for three days.

It was glorious.

The ship was mad, just pressure, claustrophobia and the constant hum of dread, split clean down the middle.

Two worlds: the sailor crew—Serbs, Croats, Romanians—and us, the hotel staff. Chefs. Bartenders. Housekeeping. Two tribes under one flag, trapped behind steel walls, bound by duty and mutual indifference.

The captain? Almost always drunk. I once watched him steer through Budapest with a whiskey in one hand and the other waving at the Parliament. A real lunatic. Flirting with female guests wasn't a scandal—it was his daily cardio. Half the sailing crew drank like the bar was on fire and they were trying to put it out from the inside. The second captain kept a full-blown rainforest in his cabin. Inside: a massive turtle in an aquarium, humidity levels suitable for a rare orchid. Algae oozed from the cracks. Passing his door felt like walking past a reptile sauna. "He's my therapist," he said once. We never asked again.

Docking days were madness. Sailors would scatter into towns the moment we dropped anchor—only to return with cigarettes, suspicious produce, or contraband. In Amsterdam, they brought back crates of strawberries and a half kilo of marijuana stashed behind a false panel in the cleaning closet. "Customs only checks tourists," one sailor said, lighting a cigarette with his shirt off. In Passau, we sometimes had real inspections—dogs sniffing every corridor. But mostly? We sailed under the radar, quite literally.

Initiations were brutal. "Going down" meant being tackled in your cabin, dragged from the toilet, and shaved bald while the crew roared with laughter. Wake up bald. Go to work like nothing happened. That's life aboard. Miss your afternoon break, and you were toast. The galley crew ran on coffee, beef drippings, and near-death experiences: breakfast and lunch, clean, prep, disappear. Nap, drink, disappear more. Then—at 4 PM—back to the galley.

The Filipino crew cooked magic in their cabins. Rice cookers on the floor. Chilies that could stun a bear. Stews, broths, sauces bubbling in recycled yogurt containers. We huddled on the floor, laughing, sweating, half-drunk on spice and exhaustion. It ruined my stomach. But my soul needed it.

The galley was fire and fury. Perfect food for people who didn't know what they were eating. Lobster tails, rack of lamb, duck confit—all delivered to guests who asked for ketchup with their filet mignon.

And of course, it wasn't just food heating up on that ship.

Hormones? Boiling. Pretty girls worked onboard. Waitresses, receptionists, housekeepers. All stuck in this floating tin can with enough men who hadn't seen their wives in six months. There was flirting over the deck, longing stares across buffet stations, and enough sexual tension to steam the windows without turning on the boiler.

One night, I passed by the crew mess—our own chaos den, part break room, part kitchen, part makeshift nightclub—and I heard it.

Moaning.

Not pain. Not hunger.

Pleasure.

Real, unfiltered, someone's-making-a-memory-tonight pleasure.

Turned out one of the sailors had his hand up a housekeeper's skirt while she clutched a yogurt and pretended she wasn't being fingered in front of a humming refrigerator and three half-empty ashtrays. They didn't stop. Just another night on the river. The crown jewel? Budapest at night. Nothing prepared you for it. Not Vienna's marble smugness. Not Cologne's gothic spires. Not even Amsterdam's gabled, weed-scented charm. This was different. Budapest glowed. The Parliament building—lit up like a palace built by phantoms—stood proud on the banks like it had witnessed too much history and wasn't done yet. Light poured off its façade like golden syrup. The Chain Bridge shimmered like something from a fairy tale about kings who drank too much and still ran empires.

Onboard, the dining room emptied. Guests stampeded to the top deck in silk scarves and windbreakers. Waiters followed with Riesling. Someone played Strauss through the speakers, like we were floating in a snow globe of nostalgia and nationalism. And the ship turned. Slowly. Majestically. Like a giant steel swan doing ballet in front of 800 years of trauma.

The bow swung wide past the Parliament, and for one brief moment—everything paused. No phones. No coughing. No clinking cutlery. Just the Danube, holding its breath. Just the lights, reflecting like molten gold. Even the old chefs poked their heads out. No one wanted to miss it.

And then— The engine kicked in. A low groan. Then a judder. Then that deep, familiar, rattling thunder that vibrated from the keel up into your teeth.

Because the ship never slept. It hummed. It shook. It quaked.

The steel floor beneath your feet buzzed like a broken massage chair. Your bunk rattled against the bulkhead like it wanted out. Sometimes you'd swear the whole thing drifted sideways—like the captain had dozed off or the Danube had too many drinks.

Then came the real horror: The turns. Sharp turns. Especially the big one, right in front of Parliament. The one that made the whole galley lurch. Plates shifted. Pans slid. One time the pastry chef's entire rack of crème brûlées took off like a missile salvo.

"Hold the panna cotta!" someone would shout—and mean it literally.

But worse than the turns? The crashes. Every season. Without fail. Sometimes twice.

Not a Titanic moment. No violins. Just… thud. Midnight or 3AM, always when you'd just fallen asleep.

BANG. A metal-on-stone gut punch that snapped you awake and launched half the crew out of their bunks.

One second you're dreaming about paprika chicken, the next you're airborne in your boxer shorts, hitting the hallway wall while an emergency exit sign swings like a drunk semaphore.

Pots fell. Knives clattered. Someone screamed. The Romanian dishwasher thought it was war. Again.

And then... silence. Like the river said, "Shhh. That didn't happen."

No announcements. No apologies.

The next morning? Breakfast. Buffet. Bacon in silver trays. Guests in polos asking for decaf and pretending they didn't fly three feet sideways in their cabin while the hull scraped the bottom like a cheese grater.

Because the river eats memory. And the ship doesn't care. It groans, it shakes, it crashes—and it keeps going. Because that's the deal. It never stops. And it never, ever stops eating its own.

Besides all this madness—if you ever wondered what made it worth it—this was the moment. And it only happened in a few rare stretches of the river.

The river narrowed. No ports. No noise. No traffic. We were deep in nature, between two villages. Just forest. Thick and endless, sloping down toward the water like it had been poured from a bucket of green. The trees leaned so far over the river their branches kissed the current. Some dragged along the surface like old witches washing their hair.

No engine roar, just a low mechanical murmur, like the ship was afraid to wake anything. The air changed. Cooler. Damp.

Clean in a way that scratched something primal. You could smell earth, moss.

Fog gathered in the bends. Low and heavy. It clung to the river like a second skin, hiding the shoreline and giving everything a floating, unfinished feel. Sometimes you couldn't tell where the water ended and the trees began. We were gliding through a painting that hadn't dried yet.

Above it all: the moon. Massive, pale, perfect. Lighting the water just enough to show the ripples—but not enough to explain them. The stars were sharp. Brutal. Too many to count. The sky didn't care who we were or where we were going.

Fish jumped. Tiny silver flashes breaking the surface in quick jolts—then gone. Maybe chasing bugs. Maybe escaping something bigger. They broke the silence with little splashes, like nature's punctuation marks.

A bell rang from the hills—soft, distant, real. One of those sleepy village churches with a bent iron clapper and chipped paint. You couldn't see the building, just feel its presence. One chime, maybe midnight. Or maybe a warning to keep moving.

I stepped outside—midnight or close. Walked to the nose of the ship, the very front deck, just to breathe.

It was stunning. The water so close I felt like I could reach down and stir it with my hand. I looked up at the bridge. The captain was there, alone. Window rolled down, cigarette dangling from his mouth, both hands on the wheel. No drink. No woman. Just him, steering this steel beast through moonlit silence. We caught each other's eyes. He raised a hand. I nodded. Nothing more. That was enough. He was enjoying it, too. He knew what this was.

And through all this? The ship—this giant metal hotel with steak knives and espresso machines—slid forward like a warship on tiptoe. Quiet. Careful. As if we weren't supposed to be there.

Just steel kissing water, barely a sound.

All slept onboard. Crew. Guests. Everyone sealed in cabins, drifting through schnitzel dreams and silent hangovers. But the river was awake. Alive in a way cities forget to be. Every bush, bird, and hidden burrow buzzing. And the ship—just this arrogant floating box—passed through it like a brief mistake in the wilderness.

No one saw it.

Except me.

And the captain. Sober.

The Staircase and the Lobster Rebellion

A loud thud, we all heard it. A sickening, final kind of sound!

We were already delayed—parked like an idiot on the riverside tarmac, engines humming, coffee cold—when word filtered down the chain: an Australian guest, elderly woman, missed a step getting off the bus. Hit her head on the cobblestone—and just like that, we had a corpse and a three-hour delay! Dead before her handbag hit the ground.

Some swore she tripped. Others whispered her husband gave her a "helping hand." He looked suspiciously calm, almost relieved, like he'd finally been unshackled from decades of loud cardigans and constant nagging.

We stood around, pretending to be sympathetic while scanning the horizon for the doctor, the coroner, the replacement bus, anything that would restart the show. Death by staircase was inconvenient. The wine delivery truck honked and left.

By the time her body was taken away, we were three hours behind schedule and everyone was sweaty, annoyed, and pretending to be somber. The husband? Back on board by lunch, ordering soup like nothing happened.

The Jumper Chef: By the third year, I became something else. A jumper—a culinary mercenary. Flown, bussed, sometimes dumped by taxi onto ships that had just lost their chef—fired, sick, dead, or AWOL. I'd step in, steady the galley, like a witness-protection chef with a knife roll. France, Germany, Netherlands. Sometimes I didn't even remember the name of the river I was on. Just a blur of stainless steel, stressed staff, and me with my knives like a medieval surgeon.

I even recruited my sister Judit for a season. Pastry chef. And damn—she was good. Calm, clever, always five steps ahead. Never whined, never broke. A rare creature in our chaos.

The Corporate Drunk: My regional corporate chef, Ringo, was a German wreck in a polyester suit. A boulder of a man with a red nose that pulsed like a warning light and a diet consisting entirely of cigarettes, panic, and potato vodka. Half-functioning brain cells barely stitched together by caffeine and whatever fumes were left in his carry-on.

Every port, he disappeared. Gone. No message. No warning. Just poof—and a few hours later he'd reappear at the gangway, dragging a duffel bag like a corpse and slurring something about "sourcing excellence." Usually drunk. Always sweating. Once he tried to board a Hungarian police boat thinking it was a tender.

He once missed the ship in Bratislava and spent six hours chasing us down the Danube in a cab—holding his crew ID out the window like a child trying to return to the circus.

But Ringo had one magic trick. One that forgave almost everything else: He got us the beef.

Not just any beef. Not "local European dry-aged whatever." Not Argentine backdoor brisket. American Black Angus—real deal, prime cuts, vacuum-sealed New York strips and tenderloins, labeled with tiny USA flags and stamps I still don't understand. Frozen, yes. But perfect. Marbled like a Renaissance painting. Rich, clean, deep red muscle. A chef's dream in a plastic pouch. I still don't know how the hell he did it. How Ringo managed to smuggle USDA beef onto a river cruise ship halfway across Europe like he was importing drugs for fine dining. You're not supposed to get that stuff here. Not without customs nightmares. Not without losing half your budget and your sanity.

But somehow, it arrived. Cases of it. Pallets. For Tauck cruises only. Because Tauck was special. Their guests weren't tourists. They were retired titans of industry who expected caviar and didn't like being told "we're out." Money was no object. And Ringo? Ringo made damn sure their last steak before death or Florida was unforgettable.

Every time I unwrapped a striploin and saw that little American flag sticker, it hit me harder than I wanted it to. That smell. That color. That texture. It was like opening a box full of memories. California kitchens. Open grills. Malibu smoke in the air. It made me homesick—for a place that wasn't even home anymore. But the meat didn't care. The meat just said, "Cook me right, and they'll remember you."

So I did. Perfect sears. Rested cuts. Clean grills. That beef never disappointed.

And neither did Ringo—when it came to the food. Say what you want about his blood alcohol content. He gave a damn about ingredients. He chased quality like it owed him money. And when you're cooking for 140 guests on a moving hotel powered by diesel and denial, you remember the people who got you the good stuff.

Ringo was chaos in a suit. But he gave us American beef in Europe. And for that? He's earned his place in this book. Right between the walk-in vodka and the night Paco pretended to die in the lobby. So I started pushing his buttons—gently at first. Then like a sledgehammer through sugar glass. It wasn't just rebellion. I was bored.

The menu had gone stale. Beef bourguignon again? I could make it blindfolded, hungover, and bleeding from both hands.

We were dragging ourselves through the tail end of a long season—guests were sleepwalking through dining room, and I was losing the will to pretend.

So I snapped.

Swapped the stew for lobster risotto with citrus foam and edible flowers. Launched unapproved amuse-bouches served under the stars, guests drifting out onto the deck in tuxedos. Moved the galley to the buffet table, made the cooks plate in front of the crowd like it was live theatre. No announcements. No permission. I flipped formats. Scrapped scripts. Treated the galley like a sandbox wired with explosives.

Because why the hell not?

The guests? They lost their minds. We weren't a river cruise anymore—we were a five-star fever dream.

The crew? They thought I was a god. Even the Filipinos—stone-faced veterans who didn't flinch at engine fires or 18-hour days—smiled like kids on Christmas when I broke protocol. I was celebrated like it was Mardi Gras every time.

We were pirates in chef whites. And for a few glittering nights, we cooked like it meant something again.

Word spread fast. Every time guests disembarked, the ratings came in—detailed, ruthless. And every time I touched a galley, that ship shot to the top. We were outscoring every other vessel—11 ships in the fleet, and mine always came out on top. Guests left reviews that read like love letters. I was building an empire.

And then… silence. I wasn't invited to the end-of-season party. No thank you, no speech, no champagne flute raised in my name.

I knew. They fired me. Cowards didn't even do it in person. But they did it wrong. I fought back. Emails. A union I tracked down. Dates. Facts.

In the end, they settled. €6,000 in compensation for wrongful dismissal. It wasn't riches—but it was enough. Enough to leave. To start again.

Next stop: Portugal. Where the pages catch fire. (And you won't believe what comes next.)

Champagne and Camouflage

When the war in Ukraine broke out, the world exploded with noise—flags on balconies, hashtags marching across social media, debates in cafés louder than espresso machines. Suddenly, being a soldier was cool, mysterious. The word "veteran" got dusted off, polished, and held up like holy scripture.

And somewhere in all that racket, I had a strange realization: I'm technically a veteran too.

Not the war-hardened, battle-scarred type. No medals, no shrapnel, no heroic last stands. The Ukraine war sent my mind back to the 90s, my army story involved a general who couldn't stand upright, a bottle of stolen champagne, and a woman named Helga who turned military discipline into a bad joke.

Let me paint the scene.

The general—his name long forgotten, but impossible to unsee—had the posture of a scarecrow caught in a storm. We'd seen him earlier that morning gripping a tree like it was about to float away. He shuffled through the grass with eyes half-closed, muttering to himself in a low, vinegary growl. The man was marinated in whatever bottom-shelf booze the officer's canteen hadn't locked up.

Then came the command: "All troops assemble! Now! In formation!"

We stumbled into the garden behind the barracks, most of us half-dressed—mismatched boots, shirts open, some still holding mugs of army tea. Uniforms were theoretical. Belts missing. Haircuts optional. The entire formation looked like a traveling circus before makeup. The general stood at the front, legs wobbling like bad scaffolding. He barked something about duty.

Honor.

Helga.

Then he swayed. Blinked. Froze. And we—all thirty of us—just started laughing. First in coughs. Then in snorts. Then full-on belly laughs. Someone lit his Camel Light. Someone else sat down. We slowly peeled off, one by one, like ice melting off a roof. The general shouted after us, slurring something about dishonor and consequences. No one listened.

That was the Hungarian military in the 1990s.

I didn't dodge the draft. My father did. Faked a medical issue and bragged about it. I wasn't going to be that guy. I reported for duty, got stationed in Budapest at Zách utca. Thanks to a well-placed csók—a connection from a neighbor with clout—I landed in kitchen duty, peeling potatoes instead of marching. Bad behavior got me promoted sideways.

First to Mátra in winter, right in the heart of ski season—perfect timing. I loved skiing. I cooked for generals who spent more time on the slopes than in strategy meetings.

Then, after another minor rebellion, they sent me to Balatonlelle for the summer—again, perfect timing. I loved Lake Balaton. Swimming, fishing, sunburns, cold beer. Winter in the mountains, summer by the lake. If this was punishment, I wanted more.

And that's where Helga entered the story. The general's daughter. Engaged. Bored. She did absolutely nothing all summer except sunbathe by the water and eat beautifully in the canteen—with the grace of a swan and the smugness of someone who knew no one would ever tell her no. She walked onto the base like trouble wrapped in sunshine. Blonde, voluptuous, confident. She had that flexible kind of beauty that made you wonder if bones were optional. I was eighteen, cocky, and allergic to rules. We were doomed from the first glance. We flirted like spies. Rendezvous behind sheds, inside pantries, between meal preps. The general turned a deeper shade of rage each day, until he practically steamed. He knew. Of course he knew. He just couldn't prove anything.

But we were done with sneak attacks. We wanted escape. Not another balcony argument or whispered breakdown in a stairwell. Real escape. Breathable air.

I dreamed of Tiszakécske—that slow, forgotten elbow in the Tisza River where time barely moved. The current there didn't rush—it paused. The water flat and warm, crowded with lilies and insects that hummed like old wires. Frogs croaked from the reeds. The world smelled like wet soil and riverbank grass. It was peace. Primitive. Untouched.

We packed light but with purpose: Inflatable flamingos, sun hats, one bottle of champagne, and two actual glasses—because if you're going to run away from capitalism, bring at least some dignity. We boarded the train like two people slipping out of their own story.

Not running. Just... leaving.

And when we arrived—sweaty, quiet, eyes wider than they'd been in months. Set up a tent in a camping. Stripped down.

Then we made love.

Fast. Then slow. Then again.

The tent rocked and moaned on its poles. It was humid and wild, skin sticking to skin like dough on a counter. Outside, frogs sang. Inside, we broke open. The mosquitoes gave up.

Beyond the nylon, the chorus kept going—low, rhythmic, indifferent. And the river didn't care who we were or what we'd done. It just held us—still, warm, anonymous.

Then the loudspeaker.

"LÁSZLÓ SZŰCS! REPORT TO BASE IMMEDIATELY OR FACE ARREST!"

The voice thundered across the campground like a NATO emergency drill. Every tent unzipped at once. Flip-flops froze mid-step. A baby started crying. Someone dropped a grill tong. A seagull flew away in protest.

The message repeated, louder this time—less command, more execution notice.

I stood there half-dressed, smelling like riverwater and sex, staring at the sky like maybe the clouds would explain how they'd found me. We hadn't told anyone. No phones. No posted photos. We'd just vanished—for not even 24 hours.

And yet here they were. Broadcasting my name like a manhunt. The entire campground was staring. Suddenly our little tent looked like evidence.

We packed in silence. Flamingo deflated. Champagne cork lost in the grass. No more frogs singing. Just the heavy thud of my pulse and the eyes of strangers judging me like I was already in cuffs.

We boarded the train sunburned, filthy, half-wild. Smug? Maybe. But also stunned. Like fugitives who only just realized the border was never real.

Back on the rails, I stared out at the Tisza, still beautiful, still slow, and thought— How the hell did they find us that fast? And what else did they know?

I had until midnight to return to base. Not metaphorically. Literally. Midnight, or military arrest.

Prison wasn't some abstract threat, whispered about in jokes or crew room fantasies. It was real. And now, it had my name printed on a file somewhere. The train rolled on. The river kept its secrets. And I started rehearsing my apology.

Just in case they didn't buy my smile.

Back at base, no words were exchanged. Just a broom. Then a pile of potatoes. Then double kitchen duty. But the punishment didn't stop there. I was shipped off to Budapest's notorious barracks—a dumping ground for misfits, thugs, and Eastern Hungarian gangsters with homemade tattoos and knife scars.

No more ski resorts. No more Balaton beaches. And no more helpful neighbors with army connections. I was in the jungle now.

Punishment? Maybe.

But I had Helga. The river. The champagne. And that loudspeaker announcement that made everyone else spit out their beer.

Veteran status? Questionable.

Story worth telling?

Absolutely.

Now... let's get back to Portugal.

Portugal or Bust – The €6,000 Gamble

Let's get one thing straight.

If you're a chef and you smoke—you've already lost the battle. No taste buds, no discipline, and fingers that smell like garlic-stuffed ashtrays. And gloves? Don't get me started. Skin gets washed. Gloves become bacteria playgrounds—touching meat, fish, then scratching your ass and tossing a salad. Grim.

Then there's alcohol. I've done my time. Oh, trust me—I earned my beer gut the old-fashioned way. Chef school started at 8 AM. The local kocsma opened at 7. We were there by 6:45—six, eight of us—lining up with local drunks and pensioners, pounding down morning misery like champions. If my mother knew? Jesus, I'd have been skinned alive with a paring knife.

First year: Vodka. Seven shots before class. Like it was part of the syllabus.

Second year: Fröccs—white wine with soda water. I could do 13 to 15 before roll call.

Third year: Beer. Just beer. And I've stayed faithful ever since. Spirits now taste bad.

So when I say I've danced with the bottle, I mean it. But I never let it own me.

Which brings us to Portugal. The Monte da Quinta Resort. A sun-baked fortress of manicured lawns, whitewashed villas, and a kitchen on the verge of cardiac arrest. The guy I was replacing? An executive chef whose face looked like a boiled beet in crisis. Red, bloated, sweating cheap gin from every pore. They said he was headed to Dubai. I say the man was one wrong breath away from a cardiac event. Either way, he was gone. And I was in. Here's the catch: it wasn't just a job. It was a rescue mission.

Terra Hotels specialized in the impossible. Scooping up bankrupt resorts, slapping on a new coat of paint, and praying it survived the season. That's where I came in. Not just to cook—but to rebuild, rewire, resurrect. A firestarter with a whisk and zero tolerance for mediocrity.

We rolled into the Algarve like cheerful anarchists crashing a billionaire's golf club. Endless rows of pristine greens, Bentleys purring at the gates, and just beyond—the Atlantic. A long, golden beach, glistening in the sun, live mussels clinging to the rocks, surf rolling in again and again, didn't know how to stop. And then—us.

We collected mussels the old-school way—barefoot, where the water met the sand. Just tapping around with our heels until we felt little clicks underfoot. They'd wriggle up—small, elongated mussels no bigger than a pinky tip. Not round and chubby like market clams, more like tiny brown capsules about 10–12 mm long—a perfect size for Mytilaster minimus.

Bucket filled fast.

Back in the caravan, we threw them into a massive pot of linguine—garlic, white wine, olive oil, and a handful of those mussels. They steamed open, spilling sweet, briny juice that clung to the pasta. We ate outside, no white tablecloths, the kind of meal that ruins restaurants. The Mercedes Vito coughed over the final hill like it was dying of tuberculosis. Behind it, a caravan held together by duct tape and prayer.

Inside:
- Janka, 3.5, running commentary on the world.
- Panka, newborn miracle, swaddled like a princess in a sardine tin.
- Kata, patient warrior, keeper of peace and snacks.
- Me. FaFa. "Wood Wood." Father, smuggler of optimism, chronic fire-builder.

We had €6,000. Severance money from a cruise ship company that dumped me like week-old scallops. We turned it into diesel, canned beans, diapers, a barely working gas heater, and just enough hope to cross Europe. Somehow, it worked.

We found a three-bedroom flat with a pool. The girls splashed in the sun. Kata breathed again. We made pasta with canned tomatoes. For a moment—it felt like a dream that hadn't turned sour yet.

But comfort is always temporary in our story.

Because just when the sun comes out—there's always a storm behind it and this day started like all hotel meetings start—inside a beige room with flickering fluorescent lights, sad coffee in plastic cups, and the German owner of Terra Hotels staring at us like we were the ones flushing his budget down the toilet.

"Electricity use... unacceptable. Paper towel consumption... excessive. Someone is stealing toilet paper!" That's when I knew we were in deep. Everyone sat there pretending to care. Eyes glazed. Croissants untouched. Gökhan, the Turkish hotel manager, looked like he'd rather jump off the balcony.

Then the big one: "One of you," the German snapped, "has been clocking very suspicious work hours. It's... highly questionable." Everyone looked around like they were waiting for someone to explode. I just kept sipping my shit coffee. Honestly, I thought he was talking about the receptionist with acrylic nails and three-hour lunches. Nope.
Turns out—he meant me. Later that day, Gökhan pulled me into a back room. Whispered, like we were about to exchange nuclear codes. "You... always clocked in, yes?" "Of course," I said. "You told me to."

He leaned in close. "That's good. Very good. They owe you over five thousand euros." I stared at him like he'd handed me a suitcase full of gold. And that's when I realized—I hadn't played the system. I'd played it too well.

The German was furious. Not because I cheated, but because I didn't. I followed the rules too precisely, and now they had to pay me. He couldn't even hide it. Avoided eye contact, muttered greetings, acted like I'd personally deflated his Audi tires. But they paid. Oh, they paid. And then came the unraveling. We were done. The dream was over.

Janka had just started school—little Hungarian girl in a Portuguese classroom, not understanding a word, but showing up every day like a goddamn warrior. And now we had to rip her out of it. We packed our life down into boxes, bags, and things we swore would be different next time. Goodbye pool. Goodbye sunshine. Goodbye built-in bathroom radios.

Kata drove the van, dragging the rusted caravan like a stubborn mule. I followed on the motorbike, my back aching, helmet fogging up. Then—middle of Spain, the kind of sunburnt, wind-sculpted landscape where car manufacturers test radiator systems—BOOM. A tyre exploded.

We pulled over. Desert heat radiating off the tarmac like a furnace. The wheel had eaten through the wooden floor of the caravan like a chainsaw on cocaine. We patched it with duct tape, leftover firewood, and blind optimism. Still moving. Still alive. Then came Bilbao—and Bilbao was... strange. We waited there in a campsite for weeks. Not entirely sure why. Maybe we needed rest. Maybe the universe needed time to catch up.

It was like the afterparty of civilization. We saw every flavor of weird. One day, a full-on domestic broke out—a woman was dragged out of a cabin by her hair, screaming like a banshee. Nobody batted an eye. Just another day in paradise. We were technically homeless. But we were not broke.

We still had enough fuel, food, and fight in us to keep going. We cooked simple food. Let the girls run wild. Watched sunsets and waited for clarity. Honestly, we had no clue where to go next. But it had to be an English-speaking country—there was no way in hell we were learning German or Spanish. French? Maybe, in another life. But we were out of time, patience, and brain cells.

So we pointed north. England.

We didn't know what was waiting on that cold, overpriced, rainy island. But at least we'd understand the signs again—and maybe even the insults.

No bosses. No screaming Germans. No whispering Gökhan conspiracies. No more basement kitchens where the only light came from the fridge.

Just the road. The girls. The wind. And whatever ridiculous chapter came next.

Welcome to England
(Now Duck)

Let's call it what it was: I stroll over to my neighbor's house. No invitation, no knock. I kick the door in, stab the husband in the chest, tell the wife she's now my property, loot the place top to bottom, then torch it for good measure — all while declaring it's for her own good. Then I paint a flag on the ruins and call it civilization.

That, in essence, was colonization.

The British were particularly good at it — polishing their boots on the backs of nations while whistling about "order" and "trade." But here's the twist: while they were busy planting Union Jacks in every corner of the globe, the Magyars — my blood, my people — were galloping west with sabers and something far older: havoc.

No apologies. No treaties. Just fire, hooves, and ambition.

Did the Magyars ever colonize England? Not quite. But they didn't have to. The wild, raven-haired riders who once threatened the gates of Europe taught the continent a lesson that empire builders often forget: fear lasts longer than diplomacy. And you can't colonize a storm.

Now, to be fair — this isn't something modern Britain is proud of. They talk about it. Often. In classrooms, in comedy, in pubs. The truth is, they know. They know their taxes fund wars they never voted for. They know the system bleeds them dry, then turns around and blames the poor.

They're not blind — just tired. And the rest of the world? Oh yeah. The world knows, too.

So here we are — centuries later — toasting civility with colonial teas, while the bones beneath our feet beg for memory. Let's dig some up, shall we? ..and somewhere in the din, I could almost hear Misci's voice from decades ago: 'Kid, the world's not broken—it's just cooking on the wrong heat. You either stir it, or it burns.

I'd grown up with the myth of Britain: politeness, order, tea — and that world-famous gentlemanly charm. You know the one: "After you, madam." "Terribly sorry." "Do come in." "Simply dreadful weather, isn't it?" "Mustn't grumble." All crisp vowels and moral superiority.

What I got instead was a pothole the size of a bathtub and a man in a purple skirt screaming at a delivery driver who had stopped in the middle of the road to argue about "respect."

We had just rolled off the Bilbao ferry in a battered caravan, the kind that rattled in third gear and smelled like wet socks and overcooked pasta left in a glovebox. I stood by the curb, road-weary and dazed, watching a bearded man in his twenties—blue sneakers, pleated lilac skirt, visible pantyhose line—waving a vape like it was a magic wand.

"You don't even know me, bruv!" he shouted, stomping in his fishnets. The taxi driver, window down, spat into the gutter and revved his engine like punctuation. That was the first five minutes. Welcome to Britain.

Next came the roundabout. An elderly woman in a Vauxhall Micra stalled halfway into a turn, hand trembling on the wheel. Cars backed up. Horns blared. A cyclist screamed "Muppet!" and kicked her fender on the way past.

Back outside, I sat on a bench, chewing a corner of a protein bar I didn't remember buying, staring at the street. A young couple kissed by the bus stop. Two men kissed harder nearby. I'd seen that before—Budapest's metro stations had their fair share of confused exhibitionists. But a sixty-year-old grandpa in a padded bra and pink-print tights, shouting into his phone about the Wi-Fi being "transphobic"—that was new. There was no warning. No slow integration. No gentle easing into modern Britain.

It hit me like a pork pie to the face.

The roads were broken. The people were louder than the traffic. It was like watching five centuries of history try to dance to dubstep.

Inside Sainsbury's, I thought things might return to normal. I was wrong.

A woman on a mobility scooter rolled by with a birdcage strapped to her shoulder like Gucci had launched a new line called 'Budgie Chic. Inside: two budgies gripping the bars like you do on a rollercoaster, cage swinging at a 45-degree angle as she bulldozed through cereal boxes and pensioners alike. She hadn't blinked since the late '80s—one of those indestructible British matriarchs forged from nicotine and spite. She wore a leopard-print fleece zipped to the neck, one sleeve halfway eaten by the cage strap. Her hair stood in wild tufts, her birds had styled it in solidarity.

Staff whispered frantically into headsets. "She's in aisle seven."

"No, wait—she's approaching feminine hygiene."

"Do we… do we stop her?"

They didn't. Nobody did. Management was paralyzed, hypnotized by the swinging cage, the tilted seed bag teetering like a fuse.

Then it happened.

Bird food detonated across the linoleum.

One budgie nearly flipped. The cage swung into a deodorant display.

A young man wearing rainbow crocs screamed and ducked behind a shelf of shampoo. The woman didn't care. She gunned it toward the self-checkout, knocking over an old man and clipping a mother's ankle on the way.

The cage, at this point, looked like it had just returned from battle. One of the birds glared at me. The other may have fainted. Customers scattered like it was an active shooter drill. Staff watched helplessly, whispering things like "Do we call corporate?" and "Can birds sue?"

We had arrived.

The Lion, the Lobster, and the Leash

We started off in a soggy campsite outside Brighton, the kind with patchy grass, suspicious puddles, and the kind of cold that clung to your bones like clingfilm. Two life-sized fiberglass cows stood at the entrance—black and white, dead-eyed, and somehow judging you. The caravan leaned slightly left. My Yamaha sat chained to a rusted fence like a loyal mutt that'd seen too much. And the Vito wheezed in protest every time we asked it to do something ambitious, like start. We searched London high and low for work—restaurants, hotels, temp agencies—but it was like trying to sell sand in the Sahara. We were either overqualified, underqualified, or just too foreign to tick the right boxes.

Then one rainy Tuesday, while trawling through Gumtree ads between bowls of instant noodles and existential dread, we saw it: "Sous Chef wanted. Fast-paced pub kitchen. Sundays are madness."

The ad didn't promise glory, but it reeked of opportunity. The Lion and Lobster. Brighton. Three floors. One kitchen.

And just like that, I was back in the fire:

Three long vans double-parked in a Brighton back alley, pissing diesel and blocking half the fire lane. The fish guy was shouting in Greek, the veg guy was late as usual, and the meat guy had blood on his boots.

Everything had to be lugged up two flights of death-trap stairs to the third-floor kitchen. The delivery guys hated it. Huffing, swearing, knees cracking like popcorn. And once they made it up? Nowhere to drop anything. Boxes balanced on bins. Fish sliding off trays. We watched them suffer like it was theatre. Perched in the attic of a 200-year-old pub like a madman in a bell tower. The Lion and Lobster. Three floors of creaking wood, crooked staircases, and floorboards that groaned like they remembered better centuries.

The whole place smelled like damp timber and overcooked ale. Part British pub, part French bistro. And on Sundays? 350 roast dinners flying out like we were feeding hungover pirates after a wedding brawl. That kitchen was a shoebox. A boiling, screaming, gloriously dysfunctional shoebox. You needed a dead man switch just to make it through Friday service. The walk-in fridge wasn't even in the kitchen. It was across the hallway, past the guest toilet. You'd be grabbing pork belly while dodging customers doing their makeup in the mirror.

The cold kitchen guy was already there—red-eyed, stoned, slicing salami with the focus of a man holding back a breakdown. His hands shook so bad we used his julienne for "rustic" garnish.

And that was before service.

But let me rewind.

My job interview with Jerone. Chef. Boss. Pocket-sized legend.

I walked in with road dust in my cuffs, Spanish heat baked into my skin, and cruise ship trauma flickering behind my eyes. Jerone stood there—still, calm, short, compact, coiled—like something that could spring or kill, depending on the order. A man of control. Another level entirely. An artist — in food and in martial arts. A little Bruce Lee in chef whites with hobbies involved danger, oxygen tanks, and maybe bullying health inspectors for sport. A man I had too much to learn from. A quiet force. Still a heavy influence, even after all these years.

No clipboard. No stupid HR questions. He looked me up and down, we chatted for about ninety seconds, then he said: "You're the guy."

That was it.

Months later, he told me: "When I saw how you looked at the stove before you looked at me, I knew."

And it's true. In this business, real recognizes real—immediately.

Exit File for the Next Chef (Classified)

To the Next Dude Who Thinks This Is Just a Cooking Gig

This ain't no welcome note. This is a survival file. Read it. Memorize it. Burn it. I left it with the butler (don't trust him either), sealed and marked "CONFIDENTIAL – FOR THE NEW CHEF'S SANITY." He promised to hand it over. If he didn't—well, you're already screwed.

Let's start at the top.

Koshi. Nice? Sometimes. Koshi is also clinically allergic to logic and lies. She calls herself "Doctor" — not medical, just academic — and runs the household absolute insane. She'll book flights for the wrong week, rent a car in the wrong name, and forget her own son at the airport. (Yes, that happened.) She's also Kumalo's assistant, which means chaos squared. Double-check everything. Triple-check the calendars.

The Money Game. They get gold mine money monthly — straight outta Zimbabwe — but it burns faster than flambéed bourbon. Rent was £27k/month in Surrey. Then couldn't afford electricity. Koshi would spend in 3 days what was meant for a month. Khosi once blew £80k on curtains. The next day, she jumped out of the car near an ATM, panicked. The card bounced. Twice. You'll be prepping filet mignon one day, then begging the butler for £20 to buy carrots the next. Plan like a doomsday chef.

Household Cast. British butler, Andy (full Downton Abbey vibes, but angrier) vs. Filipino housekeepers, Jolly on the top (stealth mode activated). It's ethnic Cold War. Passive aggression is the lingua franca.

After dinner, the housekeepers vanish. If you don't see them cleaning up the kitchen, they aren't. Get them the ironing done before 10 a.m. or you'll serve roast beef on a table that looks like laundry day. His Majesty does not dine over wrinkles — fabric or otherwise.

The Rice Cooker. It's yours. I bought it. Do not let them take it to their rooms. They'll try. Guard it with your life.

The Game Reserve. South Africa. Remote. Gorgeous. Full of landmines—literal and figurative. Forty-five minutes down a dirt road into nowhere. Get a 4x4. Trust me. Don't follow Khosi's "cheapest rental" logic—you'll end up stuck. Nine rhinos guarded and followed 24/7 by men with machine guns. One hundred and ten antelopes. Zebras. Five giraffes. No elephants—too smart for this circus.

Stock up in Johannesburg. Once you're down south, shopping is a myth. The kitchen is solid, but keep the windows closed after lunch or the monkeys will raid your mise en place. Khosi's booking skills don't improve overseas: flights booked for yesterday, rental cars on the wrong continent.

Travel with them only if you're desperate. I once drove with the butler to a Johannesburg butcher—thousands in vacuum-packed Aussie steaks in the boot—only to get trapped in a flood.

Kumalo (The King). Ex-cellmate of Mandela. First African gold mine owner. Walks like he owns everything. His African staff in the reserve bow and kiss his hand. He demands respect. Dresses like a peacock that hit the jackpot—silks, gold chains, handmade shoes polished to a mirror, cologne strong enough to evacuate a safari. Everything's a performance. He'd keep the whole house waiting for hours just to make an entrance. He's screwing the Asian masseur who comes to the house once a week.

The England Setup: They got kicked out of the Surrey house. While waiting for the Highgate mansion to be approved, we spent weeks in limbo. Somehow, they talked their way into The Lanesborough—dragging two housekeepers and a trail of unpaid bills behind them. Never paid full. Never paid on time.

Within days, the hallway stank of Jolly's midnight Asian cooking—fish sauce and fried garlic slipping past five-star wallpaper. The concierge stopped making eye contact. They tried to save money by cooking inside the hotel suite.

Highgate finally came through: £70,000 a month, bulletproof windows, somewhere near Justin Bieber's house. Still couldn't pay rent. Still forgot the traffic fines. That's when I knew—I was going to vanish.

Five-star facade. Zero-star management. All Khosi's fault.

Every.

Damn.

Time.

Pro Tips:

- Label everything. Housekeepers will raid your prep fridge.

- When they go eat to that Chinese place in London — take a day off.
- Keep emergency pasta and tinned tomatoes hidden somewhere safe.
- Don't question the zebra meat. Don't ask. Don't google. Just cook it or pretend it's bison.

Reality Check: They live like royalty, but pay like students. You'll get dragged into family drama, global logistics, shopping marathons, and weird late-night massages scheduled without asking you. The adopted son is forgotten half the time. The game reserve kills 100 zebras a day. I have questions. You will too.

Bonus Warning: Khosi will approve a lunch menu at 10 a.m., then demand goat stew by 12:15. Or worse—have you cook for six hours, full prep, plated courses… Then they cancel and go out to eat instead.

Final Thought: I stayed too long. I cooked like a missionary for a family that barely knew what day it was. Don't make my mistake. Get your pay. Keep receipts. Don't fall for the charm. This isn't a kitchen gig. It's a psychological thriller with food. Believe me.

And if Koshi hands you a booking confirmation—check the damn date.

- The Last Guy

Field Notes from KwaZulu-Natal – Service With a Side of Ammo

You don't exactly picture a chef strapping on an AK-47 when you think fine dining. But that's Africa for you—nothing predictable, especially not in the bushveld, where rhinos are worth more than gold and the menu sometimes starts with a gunshot.

They handed me the rifle like it was a spatula.

"You'll be sleeping here," said the ranger, nodding at a concrete hut the size of a coffin. "Watch out for leopards. And snakes." He let that hang in the air, then added: "Welcome to the game reserve. Chef."

The sarcasm lingered like gun smoke. I wasn't welcome. Not really. Me—the Hungarian chef. Andy—the British butler. Two white guys dropped into the middle of a heavily armed, all-African staff camp. Khumalo had hired us deliberately—to show off. He wanted a spectacle: white servants bowing to a Black king. And we felt it. Every day. Every sideways glance. Every joke we weren't part of. Every awkward silence when we walked in.

In the heart of KwaZulu-Natal, South Africa, nestled between dry savannah hills and the haunting silence of abandoned outposts, lies a private game reserve where the wild still roams under armed watch. A local ranger stands firm with a rifle slung low, a symbol of the tension between conservation and the harsh realities of protection. The reserve terrain stretches endlessly, dotted with acacia trees, rocky slopes, and dry golden grasses, where rhinos graze cautiously, giraffes silhouette against dusk skies, and zebras stripe the hillside like brushstrokes. At the center of it all is a modified game viewing vehicle, equipped with a raised tracker seat, battered but functional — a frontline tool for wildlife monitoring and anti-poaching patrols.

Poaching wasn't just a crime—it was a war. The air tasted like dry grass and burnt wood. Dust everywhere. It coated your teeth. The lodge manager—an Afrikaans guy named Koos with a beer belly—didn't greet me with a handshake. Just a nod and a machete. "You're late," he said. "Zebra got hit this morning."

We are in 2016, Zuma was still king, and the ANC—the once-sacred machine that carried Mandela's dreams—was limping on rotten legs. State capture was no longer a whispered rumor. It was breakfast conversation. Ministers with swollen pockets and greased palms. A country teetering between revolution and rot, with Jacob grinning from the top like a drunk uncle at a funeral.

But out here, in the dust-choked wilderness, none of that mattered—not to the men around the fire, certainly not to the guards watching the mountains with rifles slung low like they were expecting trouble to roll in on a Land Cruiser.

Yet, the land remembers. The soil is thick with stories—of kingdoms lost and won, of borders drawn and redrawn, of promises made and broken. The very ground beneath our boots has witnessed centuries of struggle and survival. And though the present seems detached from the past, the echoes are there, waiting to be heard.

Khumalo was old money. A Black tycoon with ties to both political royalty and hunting lodges the size of small towns. His guests arrived in convoys—SUVs blacker than night, bodyguards with sunglasses and no names. They didn't talk much. They scanned. And they waited.

Meanwhile, I cooked. Center-table grill. Flames licking steel. Smoke rising like incense for forgotten gods. Meat. Meat. Meat. Vegetables were an afterthought—garnish for the weak. What they wanted was primal: ribeye thick as a Bible, kudu loin bleeding rare, impala ribs with skin crackling like paper on a flame. Anything that once roamed and was now dead.

Andy handled the serving—white gloves, silver tongs, his face a poker mask. The man could serve a zebra steak to a minister under investigation without blinking.

Khumalo leaned back in his leather chair, belly full, fingers greasy, eyes scanning the horizon. "You know," he said, "this country runs on meat and memory." I believed him.

Days began at dawn with the Land Cruiser rumbling to life, dust clouds rising behind us like we were in a low-budget safari chase scene. On one morning, a giraffe blocked our path—majestic, indifferent, chewing lazily like it owned the damn place. And it did, in a way. Out there, the animals weren't the exhibits. We were.

And then there was the chair—bolted to the hood of the truck like a throne for the madman. That's where the rifleman sat. I tried it once. Sat up front, gun slung over my shoulder, eyes scanning for movement like I knew what I was doing. Truth is, I was a chef dressed like a soldier, playing hunter in a world where dinner could kill you back.

A zebra was strung up in the back of a transport truck, skinned halfway, steam rising from the cavity like a haunted oven. Its meat was still warm. A single bullet between the eyes. Humane by African standards. Efficient. Clinical. Koos handed me a boning knife.

"Strip the legs, avoid the guts. We feed the predators the rest."

You learn fast out there. Knives dull quickly in the heat. Flies arrive before you blink. And the sun? The sun turns blood into glue in minutes.

Skinning a zebra takes teamwork. One man holds, one man pulls, one cuts. You start at the ankles, strip upwards, and roll the hide like a rug. The ribcage is delicate. You don't want to rupture the guts—that smell will cling to your soul.

Each leg is portioned into shanks and roasts. The neck gets minced. The heart? Eaten on the spot by the ranger who made the kill—an old Zulu tradition. I tried it once. Raw, warm, metallic. Not for the faint of stomach, but symbolic. You kill it, you respect it.

Field dressing zebra isn't like cow or deer. The hide's rubbery, stubborn. You need a knife honed like a prison shiv—anything less, and you're just tickling it. The fat layer is thin, the meat dark and iron-rich. Gamey, but not foul. Somewhere between horse and antelope. The taste clings to your tongue, earthy, primal. Like something that's never seen a fence.

That night we ate zebra stew from a soot-blackened pot over an open flame. Chewy. Bloody. Honest. It paired perfectly with silence and low murmurs in isiZulu. Khumalo sat like a warlord in exile, draped in silk and sweat, watching us with that smug half-smile that said, Yes, you cook for me now.

And we did.

We fed his fantasy. Later that night, in that concrete hut, AK by the door, I stared at the ceiling fan creaking like an old confession. The butler was snoring in the next room. Somewhere outside, a hyena laughed like it knew something we didn't. And I thought to myself: Welcome to the game reserve, chef. You made it, (But at what cost). Now let's see how long you last.

I marinated the zebra tenderloin in crushed wild garlic, thyme, and Amarula—the local dessert liqueur, sweet and silky. The sugars helped break down the fibers. Then I pan-seared it over an open flame, finished it with smoked kudu fat, and served it sliced over fermented maize mash, garnished with a sprig of river mint.

There's a particular smell when zebra flesh hits hot iron—somewhere between grass-fed beef and burning tire. Not quite wild, not quite domestic. Like nature hadn't made up its mind.

The tenderloin? Koos called it "dangerous." He meant it as a compliment.

After three sleepless nights—leopards coughing outside, hyenas screeching like banshees—we tapped out. Khosi moved us to Lords of the Manor, a boutique hotel on the edge of the reserve. Crisp linens, air conditioning that didn't wheeze like a dying goat. It felt like exile in luxury.

Kudu Shank Potjiekos, we cooked it open-fire, Hungarian style, in a bogrács—a heavy iron pot hung from a chain, a cauldron, swinging just above the flames like a wrecking ball with soup ambitions.

The potjie simmered for six hours, bones poking out like they wanted to climb free. The kudu shank collapsed into strands—meaty, gamey, like lamb that grew up feral. I threw in carrots, wild garlic bulbs, and a chunk of dried mango for contrast. A glug of brandy. A handful of torn leaves from a tree no one could name. We served it thick over maize pap, the texture of wet cement and just as filling. A spoon stood straight in the bowl—and didn't dare fall.

Andy was always my first critic—my unofficial taster, food bodyguard, and bullshit detector in one. He'd test every dish before it reached the king, like a royal poison-checker from some medieval court. If his face didn't twist, if his eyebrow didn't rise, I knew I was on the right track. If he coughed, frowned, or said, "Hmmm," I'd start over.

Behind the kitchen, two massive black pigs waited like demons. We fed them everything—leftovers, scraps, bones the size of my arm. By morning, nothing remained. Not even marrow. I used to tell Andy that if Khumalo ever needed to make a chef disappear, those pigs out back would do the job in hours. No trace. No teeth. Just a squeal.

Days blurred. I stopped checking the date. Khosi ran logistics like a drunk playing darts—blindfolded. Food delayed, trucks sent to the wrong gate. We weren't just out of place. We were props—disaster relief wrapped in aprons. And the show had just begun.

Sometimes the butchering came in waves—five or six animals hung in a row, like a slaughterhouse truck had flipped over. Other times, it was quiet, eerie. You'd hear nothing for two days, then one gunshot, and the ritual would start again. There was a rhythm to it. A silence. Nobody bragged. Nobody posted pictures. These were not trophy hunters. These were working men—feeding mouths, guarding horns, holding the line between man and bush. Nothing was wasted. Not because of tradition. Because there was no backup.

This was bush kitchen theology: If you don't use it, the flies will.

And let me tell you—these weren't European flies. These bastards were airborne piranhas. Big enough to have names. Smart enough to know when meat was softest. One even flew off with a strip of fat once. I swear it winked at me.

But what stayed with me wasn't the butchering. It was the boiling.

One morning, after a night of gunshots echoing in the hills and a guard dog torn apart by hyenas, I found myself hunched over a cast-iron cauldron the size of a bathtub. Inside: zebra bones, joints, tendons, blood, water, ash—a witch's brew bubbling over wood fire.

The smell? Indescribable. Like copper coins soaked in sweat. Like wet wool roasting on a radiator. Like death trying to make consommé. I gripped the wooden paddle, shirtless—coated in zebra fat, and soap I hadn't touched in days. A ranger leaned over and muttered, "Let it reduce. Until the bones crack."

And so I did. Stirred until my shoulders burned. My own blood-soaked baptism. By the time it was done, my hands were stained, fingernails black, mind drifting somewhere between a fever dream and full-blown spiritual collapse.

The broth—thick, dark, bone-heavy—was ladled out for the night guards, who slurped it down like liquid gold. "This one make you strong," they said. "Keeps the night from swallowing you whole." No one laughed.

That night, I didn't dream. The staff radio crackled to life: "Giraffe down. Likely poachers. Move."

We found her in the tall grass, collapsed on her side—legs like felled tree trunks, eyes still blinking. Not poached for meat. Just the tail. Some believe giraffe tails bring luck or wealth. So they hacked it off and left her to die.

Koos muttered something in Afrikaans, raised his rifle, and took aim. The job wasn't culinary anymore—it was mercy. One shot. Clean.

Then more gunfire. South fence this time. The night wasn't over.

But morning came, like it always does—hot, unapologetic, and full of smoke. Outside, a woman in a headwrap fried dough balls—vetkoek—with her bare hands, shaping them as the oil popped and sang. She grinned like this was the highlight of her week. Maybe it was.

Her name was Thandeka, her thick forearms flexing with rhythm, eyes half-closed as though she were praying. The pink plastic bowl never left her side. Neither did the dough. She worked it until it surrendered. She dropped the dough into the scalding fat, and it puffed up instantly into something golden, blistered, tender. It was called vetkoek — fat cake. A deep-fried miracle.

Thandeka didn't work for the kitchen. She didn't work for anyone, really. She served. She ironed shirts for the king when he flew in from wherever kings fly in from. She cooked for the rangers. She swept the concrete dorms, washed everyone's socks, folded my uniform with the kind of care I didn't deserve. And she smiled. Always smiled. I saw her on those mornings, hunched over a steel basin in the laundry hut, humming while she scrubbed Khumalo's underpants. Or in the fire kitchen, barefoot, stirring pap with a stick like a witch conjuring something or fighting fire. I wanted to help. I didn't. Not then. I had my white coat. My ego. My deadlines. Zebra shank to braise. Politicians to impress. I didn't make room for her story. But it followed me.

She came from the highlands of Lesotho—where the air is thin, the land is carved from stone, and villages grip the mountaintops like hands refusing to let go. No bus. No taxi. Just her feet on the tar. Sometimes in cracked boots. Sometimes barefoot.

Three days of walking—because even if a bush taxi passed, she couldn't afford the fare. Trucks screamed past, and if she was lucky, one might stop. Most didn't. So she kept walking. Not like a beast of burden, but like a woman who knew the world wouldn't come to her. She left her children behind. Even the newborn. Her husband stayed home—half-drunk, bitter, refusing to lift a finger for work. She crossed the border. Crossed the mountains. Because someone had to feed them. Out here, survival didn't ask for permission. It just watched who moved and who didn't.

We butchered zebras by the dozen. One hundred in a week. I sliced meat until my arms ached. Zebra skins were salted, stacked, and sold—destined to become rugs in some dictator's lounge. The blood soaked into my chef whites and seeped into the stories I still carry today.

I posed for a photo—AK-47 in hand, chef jacket on, the look of a man who's both lost and found something deep in the heart of Africa. The camera clicked—and that version of me was sealed forever. A place where the rules didn't apply. Where a Hungarian chef could be a gunman, giraffes had right of way, and you learned to cook with your back to the wild. They don't teach you this in culinary school. But damn, they should.

After moving through so many countries, I kept asking myself: Which place do I miss the most? Not the easiest. Not the richest. Not the safest.

I miss the place where I felt free. Brutal. Beautiful. Real. And that place... is South Africa.

Every return was harder. Every visit left a mark. There were days I didn't feel safe— faces I couldn't read, tension like static in the air. But somehow, I felt more myself there than anywhere else. Now, after fifty years on this planet, I finally get it: I don't miss comfort. I miss places that woke me up. And freedom—true freedom—changes your shape.

Permanently.

Fish Bones and Stolen Statues

London, Mayfair. Private townhouse. Three-storey Georgian monument to power. Everything reeks of polish and performance. I'm standing in a marble kitchen the size of a Balkan apartment, wrist-deep in the belly of a sea bass so fresh it still twitches in my hand.

Across from me? A glass cabinet of kidnapped gods—Benin bronzes, masks from Mali, spears that once roared over open savannahs.

The owner, Nigel—mid-60s, teeth too perfect for someone without a soul, money from oil or arms or something less polite—glides in wearing slippers stitched from extinction.

"Chef, any chance we can have it mild? No spice tonight."

Mild. Of course. The colonizer's palate.

I don't answer. But in my head: Sure, sir. Just a pinch of paprika—Hungarian diplomacy.

Instead, I gut the fish and stare into its vacant eye, wondering which empire swallowed it first.

Colonial powers didn't conquer for flavor—they craved control.

And now, I'm stuffing rosemary into a corpse while pieces of plundered Africa hang behind UV glass like trophies.

England, what a place. Rich in history! Confident too. Castles, manor houses, and abbeys — well, bits of them. Dismantled by monarchs, bombed by the Germans, or simply abandoned when the cost of keeping a butler outpaced the family cocaine habit. These places are everywhere. Perched on cliffs, buried in hedge-lined estates, now repackaged as National Trust "experiences." For a yearly fee, you can stroll through as many as you like.

I visited some. One had a moat and a falconer giving a talk about medieval hunting while bored kids threw crisps at a peacock. Another had a café where you could eat an overpriced scone on the ruins of a 14th-century abbot's quarters. They press apples fresh for juice — 5L, 10L containers, or straight to your reusable hipster bottle if you ask nicely.

And the gardens — credit where it's due — are immaculate. Landscaped to within an inch of godliness, ancient yew mazes trimmed tighter than a Buckingham buzzcut. Some of the buildings are restored so well you almost forget how much blood and fire it took to raise them in the first place.

But the history? That's the trick. The plaques talk about "Sir Edward Witherspoon, Member of Parliament, industrialist." What they skip is that his fortune came from sugar plantations in the West Indies — run on slave labour whose names never made it into the family Bible. Or that the hand-carved oak panels in the drawing room came from Congolese forests, logged with bullets and bribery. Or that the silverware gleaming under soft museum lights was paid for by opium sold to the Chinese, or rubber pulled from colonial Congo, or corpses in the wrong colour. Still — some of these places are breathtaking.

The light hits old stone just right in the evenings. The air holds a kind of hush. Not peace. Power cooling off. You feel it under your feet. Something built to last. They've turned all this into an attraction now. Pay fifteen quid, walk through generations of loot, buy some fudge. A tea towel with Henry VIII on it. Maybe a fridge magnet of the guillotine that never came.

If you want to see the same logic exported, look at the Getty Villa — that opulent replica of a Roman estate up in the hills of Malibu. Built by an oil tycoon. Stuffed with Greek and Roman art "acquired" under circumstances polite society doesn't ask about.

Aphrodite, a towering goddess looted from a Sicilian ruin, shipped across oceans to stand serene by the Villa's herb garden. You sip iced coffee next to statues torn from sacred ground, packed into shipping containers at gunpoint.

In South Africa, I visited a Cape Dutch estate once owned by a diamond baron who went mad and drowned in his own bathtub. These days it's a boutique winery with a peacock problem and a fusion tasting menu. Locals say it's a shining example of post-apartheid reuse. But when you scratch the surface, it's still dressed-up colonialism.

The kitchen offered biltong pâté on brioche with mango chutney, plated fancy. The chef was white, trained in France. The waiters weren't.

Back in England, the aristocracy didn't vanish — it just rebranded. Now it wears linen and runs Instagram accounts about preserving "historic homes." The same families that once taxed the villagers into starvation now charge £9.50 to look at a four-poster bed. And if you act suitably impressed, you can even sleep in it — honeymoon package included. Just don't ask where the money came from. Or whose backs paid for it.

But the castles?

Still standing.

Still beautiful.

Still selling tickets.

Still telling half the story.

Absence in White Gloves

The fire snapped like bones breaking. Dry acacia crackled in orange bursts, casting a shaky circle of light in the ocean of black that swallowed the bush around us. Beyond that ring: nothing but stars, silence, and the occasional low growl that reminded us we weren't alone.

Andy sat across from me, Lion Lager in hand, sweat-drenched shirt clinging to his back. Neither of us said much. We weren't here to talk. We were here to listen, on our fifth trip. In Africa we truly loved.

Three rangers sat with us in the sand—silent silhouettes most of the day, but different now, their rifles resting against a log like sleeping dogs. The youngest, David, maybe mid-twenties, had a fresh scar running down his jawline. Still had some softness in his eyes, not yet hollowed out by too many years on patrol.

Next to him, Joseph—older, with calloused hands stained from grease and gun oil, fingernails black with bush dirt. His boots were cracked at the toe, and he sat cross-legged in the sand like a man who'd been sitting in this dirt his whole life. He spoke slow, each word weighed before release. You could tell he'd buried friends. Probably more than once.

The third—just called himself Moses—didn't speak at first. He stared into the fire, lips barely moving, like he was praying or counting sins. When he finally spoke, it wasn't a voice—it was a scarred drumbeat. His words about colonialism lingered, pulling me back to the wounds I'd seen etched into Africa's skin.

"People think colonialism ended," he said, tossing a small branch into the fire. "But look around. The theft never stopped."

Andy and I exchanged a glance. We said nothing.

Joseph picked up where Moses left off, pointed a cracked finger toward the trees. "You see those forests out there? Protected, once. Now they've been sold off. Chopped. Gone. Sold with forged deeds. Same system. New hands."

His voice didn't rise, but the fire seemed to.

Andy's voice cracked as he finally spoke. "So what do we do?"

No one answered.

The fire roared for a moment as a log collapsed inward. Then Joseph said, "You don't bury the truth. You carry it. You speak it. Loud. Until it burns through the lies."

A hyena whooped in the distance. Everyone looked out past the firelight, toward the shadows.

"We good?" David asked, lifting his rifle gently.

Moses smiled. "We're always good. Until we're not."

We sat a while longer. The fire died slowly, but the heat of the stories didn't. Andy and I lay back in the sand, staring at the stars. I've seen both. The castles, the cream teas, the restored manor houses peddling "heritage." And the other side — rusted oil rigs, looted land, and nations still bleeding from what Europe called progress. One half of the world sells scones in rooms built on empire. The other half is still paying the bill. Welcome to Africa's underbelly — oil-soaked, plunder-scarred, and anything but history.

Congo. Kenya. Not the past. They are still happening.
Let's start with Congo, if you're hungry for truth. If Hell had a regional franchise, it would've been the Congo Free State under King Leopold II — 1885 to 1908. The Belgians didn't colonize. They extracted. Rubber. Ivory. Lives. Their business plan? Pure horror, sold with royal seals.

Now, you may not know William Lever — but you probably know Unilever. Soap empire. Household name. Built not in Liverpool, but in the Congo, and not on innovation, but on blood. His operation, Huileries du Congo Belge, sounds like a luxury chocolate brand. It was a forced labour mill. Palm oil wasn't harvested. It was ripped from jungle and body alike.
Children watched their parents mutilated when quotas weren't met. That oil greased the wheels of European hygiene.
By 1911, Lever Brothers controlled 750,000 hectares of plantations.

The Force Publique — Belgium's colonial police — kept the whips cracking and the numbers up. Villages burned. Whips made from hippo hide. Terror dressed as trade. This wasn't business. This was industrialized cruelty. And the world? Didn't scroll past — it never even saw it. No social media. No watchdogs. Just newspapers edited in drawing rooms owned by the same families profiting off it all.
Independence eventually arrived. Fake freedom with a side of debt. In 1969, Congo-Brazzaville struck oil — vast offshore fields near Kouilou.
Today, oil makes up more than 80% of its exports. Yet over 70% of Congolese live in poverty. Where did it go? Swiss traders like Glencore and Gunvor secured sweetheart deals through contracts signed behind smoked glass. Billions

disappeared into shell companies. The state oil firm, SNPC, became a black hole.

Hospitals ran without anesthesia. Children died of malaria. Meanwhile, oil executives booked first-class seats to Geneva and poured Château Margaux over ice. Lusanga — once called Leverville — is now a carcass. The factories are dead. The wealth is long gone. But the pipelines? Still running. Still silent. Still making someone, somewhere, very rich.

And then there's Kenya. The British empire looked at the highlands and saw paradise — as long as your skin reflected sunlight. They called it the White Highlands, all 7.5 million acres of it. Free land. No remorse. Just inherited theft, passed down like furniture. Colonial administrators said its "development." It was conquest, in fountain pen ink. Lord Delamere took over 100,000 acres.

The locals? Slaughtered. In 1905, the British led the Sotik Massacre, killing up to 1,850 Kipsigis people. A "punitive expedition." Translation: ethnic cleansing in uniform. By 1948, 30,000 white settlers owned nearly all the usable farmland. Africans were herded into "Native Reserves" — 7% of the land for 90% of the people. Independence followed. Flags. Anthems.

And the land? It didn't go back. It moved sideways — from colonial aristocrats to post-colonial presidents and their cousins. The Ndungu Commission laid it bare in 2004: 200,000 illegal titles.

National parks. Forests. Rivers. Carved up and sold off. From empire to elite — same dinner party, different guest list. Today, 20% of Kenyans control 80% of the land. The rest inherit dust and drought. Take the Wakasighau. Evicted during World War I. Shipped to Malindi. No return. No restitution. Just silence passed from parent to child like an heirloom.

Now the West wants closure. So they send diplomats and damp-eyed apologies. They say "sorry" — from manicured verandas on stolen earth. But if you're still living on what was taken? Your sorry means nothing. This chapter isn't about guilt. It's about debt.

When the colonizers packed up, they didn't disappear. They diversified.
From rifles to contracts.
From settlers to shareholders.
From blood to balance sheets. And no — these aren't ghosts of colonialism.
Ghosts don't sign oil deals or run hedge funds.
These are systems.
Pipelines.
Boardrooms built on conquest. Fences backed by law and silence. So don't soften it. Don't poeticise it. This isn't a whisper. It's a bill. Long overdue. Still climbing. And the truth? It never dies. It just waits — beneath the oil, behind the hedge fund — for someone to light a match.

The game reserve, the guns, the drama, Khosi's layers of insanity—it had been another world. And like all the others before it, we packed it into memory and moved on.

We weren't running this time, just shifting, looking for a pause. A quieter insanity.

Andy wasn't just a memory. He became a friend. A regular guest in our home in Brighton. Trusted enough that by Christmas 2017, he was house-sitting for us—feeding the cat, boiling his endless kettle, quietly adjusting things he believed needed correcting.

He talked often about a new job. Something "financial." Discreet.

"Asset movement across sensitive borders," he said. "For high-value clients."

We asked, "What kind of clients?"

He squinted like he was checking for bugs and said: "Russians."

And that was that. No explanation. No details. Just Andy in his shiny black sneakers, belly hanging confidently over his waistband, sipping tea with milk like he was running a covert embassy from our dining table.

You could sit down with Andy and get a full hour of grievances:

- The Filipino staff had turned mind games into an Olympic sport
- Khosi made decisions that defied logic, consistency, basic human dignity—and occasionally human rights
- Discipline was dead, and the Queen had declared war on common sense

But the scar he picked at every time, was that cursed road trip. Jolly and Andy had been arguing in the car for hours. Something small that became everything. The tone. The look. The placement of a bottle—who knows. Then Jolly began her silent protest. And Andy unraveled.

We were somewhere between Johannesburg and Mooi River when we pulled over for petrol. Stretched our legs. Grabbed snacks. Refilled coffee. Jolly stayed in the back seat. Jacket over her head. Stone silent. Wouldn't get out. Wouldn't eat. Wouldn't speak. We drove off, full bellies, coffee in hand. Later—of course—Jolly told Khosi we never stopped. That she asked for a toilet break. For food. That we ignored her. Classic victim theatre. The backstabbing games were next level. Andy couldn't get over it.

"She weaponized the silence," he said. "Do you understand? It was planned."

Every time he brought it up, I just nodded. By then, I was already wondering how the man who once served lamb to politicians became a walking financial hallucination.

Then came the trunk.

Andy stepped outside and waited. "I want to show you something," he said—voice low, grave. Like we were about to dig a hole and never speak of it again.

He led me to his black BMW. Gleaming. Quiet. Sinister. The kind of car that doesn't park—it stakes out.

He looked both ways. Then opened the boot. He lifted a thin grey blanket. Stacks. Bundled black paper. Wrapped clean. Packed wall to wall, from corner to corner. Like printer paper made for crime.

"Don't touch it," he said.

He leaned in. "This is secured currency. Dyed black to cross borders. Real money. Just needs cleaning."

Then he dropped the blanket and closed the boot slowly, scanning the street like someone might already be coming.

I stared at him. He stared back. I went inside. Sat down. Searched it.

Black Money Scam. Wash-Wash. Trunk Trick. It was all there. Word for word. The pitch. The paper. The fake embassy story. The "cleaning solution" you buy for a few grand to wash your way to fortune. The solution. The promise. The disappearance.

I showed him the results. He didn't react.

"That's disinformation," he muttered, and turned away.

A week later, he said he had a delivery. "Quick trip," he said. "France."

That was the last time we saw Andy. No message. No call.

No postcard from Paris. Gone.

The Other Knife in the Kitchen

Barefoot kid stirred the stew with a broken plank, eyes half-closed from the woodsmoke. The pot sat on bricks, blackened by years of fire, bubbling over with goat bones, rust-colored broth, and dried fish heads staring back like half-sunken wrecks. Flies danced at the edges of the smoke. A radio crackled something about Manchester United. Behind him, the wall was tagged with peeling posters for lost elections, Coca Cola and umqombothi. Next to him, an uncle in a sleeveless vest chopped onions on a crate that once smuggled Belgian rifles. The blade was dull, the onions small, but the rhythm was perfect. A dog scratched itself in the dirt.

A girl walked past balancing water container on her head like a crown. No running water. No fridge. But damn if the food didn't smell like heaven dipped in diesel.

It wasn't much, but it fed ten mouths and one stray dog.

And while all this bubbled under the African sun, air-conditioned men half a world away, inside a sealed-off nerve center chilled to a corporate 20°C, wrinkle-free shirts sipped Nespresso and snacked on shrink-wrapped protein bars. The buzz of high-speed printers harmonized with the click of polished Oxfords across epoxy floors. From behind fingerprint scanners and biometric doors, they approved containers of powdered eggs from Denmark, shelf-stable milk from Bavaria, dehydrated soup mix from Iowa, and peanut paste engineered to last longer than most marriages.

The mango hanging outside the village hut? Too organic. Too unpredictable. No barcode, no corporate middleman, no kickback. It didn't exist.

Ever wonder why that is? Why it's damn near impossible to find real food in half of Africa's small towns? No fresh fish. No raw milk. No good meat unless you know a guy with a machete and a cow. Just canned, boxed, frozen crap — like flavor's been outlawed. Ask the CIA. No, not the butcher, not the bureaucrat, not even the bishop. Ask Langley. John Stockwell did.

He was Langley, running black operations across continents like some twisted maître d' of mayhem. He didn't serve food—he served coups, sabotage, disinformation. "We killed six million people in the Third World, all to protect the 'national interest,'" he said in 1987, like a chef announcing how many lobsters he slaughtered for a dinner service. Except these weren't crustaceans. These were people. Black, brown, poor, and inconvenient.

Stockwell wasn't some conspiracy theorist holed up in a shack. He was Chief of the CIA's Angola Task Force, sent to destabilize a left-leaning African country after Portugal's colonial grip finally slipped. Angola was finally free—until the Cold War rolled in like a meat truck. The U.S. backed two proxy forces—UNITA and FNLA—against the MPLA, who were winning support not just from the Soviets and Cubans, but the Angolan people. So the CIA did what it does best: sowed chaos.

The blood? Outsourced. The truth? Buried in disinformation campaigns fed to both American and African media. CIA officers created fake press releases, conjured up Soviet troop sightings, and bribed journalists in Zambia, Zaire, and back home. One of their tactics was to forge MPLA death lists, leaking them to newspapers to justify support for the rebels. It wasn't just war—it was performance art, with bullets instead of reviews.

Africa was never just a Cold War chessboard—it was a buffet for the imperial elite. And the CIA was the sommelier, pairing coups with trade deals.
Ghana, 1966—Kwame Nkrumah overthrown after flirting too hard with socialism. Congo, 1961—Patrice Lumumba tortured, shot, and dissolved in acid while CIA cables winked approval. Zaire's Mobutu pocketed $150 million in U.S. cash while his people drank diesel-tainted puddles. Ethiopia—backed Selassie for decades, dropped him when he was useless. South Africa—helped track Nelson Mandela in 1962, then later polished the statue.

The blood was outsourced, the truth buried in fake Soviet troop sightings, forged death lists, and journalists bribed from Lusaka to D.C. John Stockwell, once Chief of the CIA's Angola Task Force, admitted to 3,000 covert operations between WWII and the '80s—most of them psychological warfare, market sabotage, or flat-out lies. "Secret wars are not secret," he said. "They're just not reported."

They didn't just kill people—they killed hope.

They destabilized governments, planted fake letters allegedly from Soviet embassies, and poisoned crops when subtlety failed. In Mozambique, in Sudan, in Namibia—Africa bled while Wall Street rose.

And the most brutal irony? They claimed it was to stop communism. But communism, at least in its naïve African form, meant land redistribution, food programs, and education. The kind of things a young African could believe in. That's what the CIA killed—not just people, but hope. Stockwell left the CIA and wrote In Search of Enemies. He wasn't just searching for foreign ones—he was naming the domestic ones who wore suits and spoke of freedom while igniting civil wars.

He ended his speech with a warning. "We must stop these wars, or we will destroy ourselves." He was talking about America. But he could've been talking about the world. About Africa. About the food missing from the plate and the ghosts still whispering over unmarked graves.

The barefoot kid with the stew? He'll grow up thinking scarcity is natural. He'll never know it was manufactured.

Peacehaven – The Town Time Forgot

We landed in Peacehaven—seaside England, grey and gnarled—where the wildest creature was a fox and the greatest threat was an 89-year-old reversing without looking. Janka and Panka swapped schools, trading Brighton's buzz for Peacehaven's sleepy cliffs. Kata unpacked boxes with the numb precision of someone who's done it too many times—over the years, we've moved so often it's muscle memory.

And me? I started noticing the birds. The coughs. The slow burn of a town that had stopped moving but still hadn't shut up.

Welcome to Peacehaven: where motion's rare and rage is heritage. The kind of place where time tripped over a mobility scooter in 1967 and never got up.

It's technically a seaside town, but don't be fooled. Yes, the sea's there—technically. But no sunbathers, no surfers. You'll be lucky to spot a fisherman. What you will see is a maze of one-way streets to nowhere. Delivery vans doing three-point turns. Roads so tight the garbage truck has to reverse half a mile. Every other sign reads "No Through Traffic," "Road Closed," or "Access Only"—as if the town was designed by someone halfway through a nervous breakdown. Half the streets lead nowhere. The other half lead to another street that also leads nowhere. This isn't urban planning. It's a cry for help.

The people? Old. Slow. Angry. I've never been anywhere else where I saw someone yell at a bird.

The streets are ruled by the barely alive. Every day, some pensioner folds over the steering wheel and forgets why they were driving—or drives with the aim of reaching the afterlife. Brake lights flicker with the rhythm of early dementia. Crosswalks are a gamble. And the mood—God, the mood. The default setting here is "grumpy with a side of suspicious." Walk into a shop and say "Good morning," and they'll look at you like Jesse James just announced a bank heist mid-brunch.

And nowhere captures the horror like the Peacehaven Post Office. I went in once. It was dead quiet. But not empty. Oh no—full of people standing still, like they'd been installed there. The woman behind the glass had the emotional range of a broken radiator.

Then it happened. The Cough.

An old man bent over near the newspaper rack. Question-mark shaped, wrapped in the same overcoat since Thatcher's funeral. He reached for a Daily Mail and—coughed.

No. Not a cough. He detonated.

It came from somewhere deep and wet, a rattling eruption that echoed off the walls. A foghorn made of phlegm. It went on so long I began to think it might be infinite.

The room froze. People turned slowly. A child whimpered. A stamp book hit the floor. One old woman clutched her heart. I swear the air changed. He straightened like nothing happened. Wiped his lip. Grabbed his paper. Shuffled off—leaving behind an invisible cloud of ancient bacteria.

I walked out without posting anything. Whatever it was, it could wait.

Here, no one minds their own business. You could be breathing like a decent human and someone will still find a reason to pull over and scream at you.

But that's Peacehaven. The seagulls get more judgment than tax fraud. The foxes? Straight-up despised.

And yet—how can you hate a fox? God made them with smiling faces, that perfect little white line around the snout. They look like they just heard a brilliant joke and are too polite to repeat it. Sleek. Clever. Playful. A thousand times more graceful than half the town's drivers.

We feed them and care for them. Watch them trot through the night like elegant thieves. And if that makes us outcasts, so be it.

Welcome to Peacehaven. The town where nothing happens fast, but everything's somehow already too late. A seaside village with no sailors, no surfers, no swimmers—just the long, slow drowning of a country forgetting how to live. Where the only traffic is memory loss—and everyone's stuck behind it, honking through dementia.

So that's where it ended—on the edge of England, in a crumbling town called Peacehaven, staring out at a gray sea that didn't care who I was. The kitchen burns had healed. The scars were mostly invisible now. The hunger never left.

If you've come this far—you've walked with me through grease, ghosts, guts, and greatness.

Thank you. You've survived the burn. You've tasted the blood. You've laughed when you probably shouldn't have. And if this book did its job—you're a little hungrier now.

For truth.

For flavor.

For a life without filters.

The story's been told. So go ahead—chop louder, drink deeper, burn brighter. Life's not a recipe. It's a fire. And you, my friend, were born to face the heat.

But wait—

Thought that was the end?

Hell no. I've got one more for you. One last ride. One perfect day. One kitchen where everything—finally—clicked.

Every great meal deserves a final course. And this one? It comes with the highest stakes I've ever served. Horses thundering past. Nobles watching.

Flip the page. The Bonus Chapter awaits.

Final Flame for The Looted Plate

I stepped to the edge of the tiny kitchen, holding the thermometer like a detonator—one degree off, and the illusion explodes. Beyond it, the gleaming prep sanctuary inside Lady Elizabeth Anson's private box—a room engineered for calm, wired for elegance, where expectations simmered. Timing could crown—or kill.

This wasn't a dining room. It was a sealed realm of privilege, tucked behind cream curtains thick as opera drapes and gold handles warm to the touch. A money-soaked fairytale. Crimson velvet thrones stood in formation around a mahogany table so polished it reflected a world where nothing was earned, only passed down. Oil paintings of horses, framed in gold-leaf, seemed to snort and twitch with aristocratic fury—stallions immortalized mid-victory, their eyes still wild.

Crystal decanters sweated quietly, chilled from cellars older than empires. They stood guard beside fruit engineered to impress God. Every strawberry was a sculpture. The grapes looked imported from a vineyard that doesn't exist on maps. Beyond the glass wall, the view spilled over the grandstand—a living painting soaked in heat and horsepower.

The turf shimmered under sunlight like it had been ironed by cherubs. And out there, the world had dressed itself in silk, champagne, and old family names, still pretending it ran on class instead of capital. Couples drifted through the grass as if they'd bought the land that morning. Security loomed motionless, eyes behind mirrored shades, scanning a crowd where no one looked dangerous—but everyone was. In their own way.

"And now—into the final furlong—Enable still leading, Ulysses chasing hard—can she hold on?!"

The announcer's voice cracked over the speakers as the crowd surged to its feet. The Royal Enclosure came alive—hats swaying, champagne sloshing, the roar building like a wave.

Enable, the three-year-old filly, elegant and ruthless, surged forward with that impossible lightness she was known for. Dettori crouched low in the saddle like he was carving wind. Ulysses gave chase—muscle and pedigree in full stretch.

"Enable by two lengths—she's done it!"

Cheers exploded. Cigars lit. A record shattered. A filly crowned.

Ascot, King George VI and Queen Elizabeth Stakes, July 2017 — a four-course feast for twenty-two guests: nobles, bluebloods, financiers, a duchess or two. Every fork served a dynasty, every glass toasted an agenda. Grass that had never known a footprint without pedigree. Threads of old money and empire stitched through every bite—you could taste the legacy in the jus. And one Saudi sheikh, still en route — his name whispered, arrival indefinite, the place at the head of the table polished like prophecy. Rumour said he might land on site by helicopter.

You ever stop mid-sauce, elbow-deep in veal stock, and think—the only reason half the Western world can afford truffle risotto is because Africa got strip-mined like a copper buffet?

Never mind! Five Chateaubriands hissed on the cast-iron like silk being torn by a tiger—dry-aged, grass-fed Dexter, the Rolls Royce of beef—slow-raised on rich English pasture, rarer than Angus, and favoured by a few aristocratic estates.

No talking. Just silent choreography. One misstep and you'd be banished to the cloakroom in Kazakhstan, and let me tell you...You don't come back from that.

I had ninety seconds to sear before the smoke alarm joined the guest list. Extractor fans on full blast. Doors cracked. Towels swinging. After that—no smoke, no scent. Just precision. But first, let me explain why working in a cloakroom in Kazakhstan is hell on Earth.

See, in Kazakhstan, the cloakroom wasn't optional—it was law. You could walk in with a bear on your back, but you'd better hang it up before stepping into the classroom or the babushka at the door would erase you from existence with one glare. Cloakrooms were state-controlled checkpoints patrolled by pensioners with steel nerves and thermal socks. These weren't coat check ladies. These were coat commandos.

Think Soviet-era vestibule the size of a broom closet, packed with 600 soggy winter coats, parkas, puffers, trench monstrosities each dripping. No heating, no ventilation—just wet wool went to ferment. Kids shoved their gear at you like they were tossing meat to a guard dog, and when one went missing, they didn't blame the kid who forgot it—they blamed you. You didn't work the cloakroom. You survived it. Which is why, when I say ninety seconds to sear the tenderloin under royal pressure was relaxing, I mean it. At least meat doesn't scream. This wasn't lunch—it was a power ritual where no one ate until the prince signaled the start. The menu was dug from the Anson family archive, transcribed in faded ink on heavy parchment—unearthed by a private secretary who once served tea to the Queen Mother.

Passed down. Preserved. Untouched by time. But here's the twist: it said Jacob's Ladder.

Jacob's bloody Ladder. Not Chateaubriand. Not tenderloin. Not the glistening filet I had seared—resting and ready—on my board.

Someone—printer, planner, saboteur—had decided we were doing heritage short ribs tonight. The slow-braised, bone-heavy kind that takes six hours, a bottle of Barolo, and the kind of patience usually reserved for hostage negotiators. But the tenderloin was already in motion. There was no going back. So I plated a lie and prayed no one knew the difference. They didn't. One guest said, "Takes me right back to my grandfather's game dinners."

Yes, darling. Granddad slow-roasted filet mignon while foraging for pheasant in tweed trousers. Yes, Karen—I'm sure your 19th-century coal-miner grandfather slow-braised Chateaubriand on Sundays between shifts.

A quiet fraud. The kind that makes you wonder how much of fine dining is really just illusion for people who never look too closely. A culinary crime—not because I cut corners, but because I didn't. I gave them better than they asked for. And in this business, that's the most dangerous mistake of all.

The prince's chair sat empty— anchoring the table, an altar of authority, a throne awaiting power itself. Outside, the Royal Enclosure unfurled like a costume drama in real time. The main grandstand towered a palace stacked with petro-gold and hedge fund voodoo. A sweeping glass façade swallowed the skyline, curving like a modern cathedral. They say it's one of the largest structures in Berkshire—half a kilometre long. But it wasn't the size that stunned you. It was the shine.

I moved through the room unseen, unheard, but absorbing everything. I watched millionaires bluff sincerity, hedge funders flirt with MPs' wives, and one old man — probably old enough to remember Churchill — whisper to his grandson, "We used to own land in Kenya, you know. 10,000 acres. Paid nothing for it." He said it like it was something noble. Something earned. That line stuck with me. "We paid nothing for it." That wasn't wealth. That was theft.

Glamis Castle pancakes opened the show — a nod to heritage, I suppose. They'd supplied me with some French pre-made crêpes from the store — trash quality, if you ask me. Straight into the bin they went. I made my own from scratch. I tasted them, naturally — delicate, precise, pretentious. Pancakes, yes, but not the kind your nan flips on a Sunday morning. These came with a title, expected a standing ovation — thin, almost translucent, cooked on a perfectly seasoned iron griddle until gold. Each was folded like a letter from a long-lost relative.

No syrup drowning the plate, no rushed butter melting in puddles — just that elegant balance of flavor and texture. A nod to centuries of expectation: savory galettes, thin and pliable, folded over melted Cheddar and chives. All hush before the storm of meat to come.

A quick pancake batter isn't rocket science, but it's a delicate dance. Start with two eggs cracked into a bowl, three generous tablespoons of flour sifted through a tamis to keep it light, and a splash of milk. Mix it hard — no gentle folding here — because the friction wakes up the flour and helps break up any lumps early on. Getting it moving fast from the start means the batter will be smooth and silky, without those annoying pockets of dry flour that never quite disappear.

Then add a tiny pinch of baking soda, followed by a splash of soda water to give the batter a subtle fizz and lightness. A pinch of salt balances the flavors. After that, slowly add more milk to bring the batter to the perfect thickness — thin enough to spread easily in the pan but thick enough to hold its shape. Finally, let it rest for a bit, then give it one last brisk stir before sliding it onto the griddle.

Behind the scenes, the kitchen was a temple of precision. Every pan gleamed as if freshly minted. Every surface wiped down before the next move. No crumbs, no smudges. I kept the kitchen immaculate, knowing the room beyond the curtain watched, waiting for perfection.

Then came the grass-fed Dexter. Rich, arrogant, like the crowd. The star, of course, was the perfect sear: dark caramelized crust giving way to blushing pink meat. That edge — that whisper-thin band between crisp and rare — took obsession. After roasting, rested above the oven, where the fading heat worked as planned, between iron and flesh. Just before carving, it went back into the hot box — not to cook, but to wake up. Then came the cut: juicy, precise, unapologetically pink. It landed on gold-rimmed china, the kind kept behind glass when emperors visit. Preheated, of course — no lukewarm sins here. On that glowing porcelain, the thick, tall beef sat like royalty flanked by its guards: piped celeriac purée and raked mustard mash, each line holding firm like starch on parade. The colors, the geometry — it was edible architecture.

Then the silver cloches came down with a soft clink, sealing the heat, sealing the moment. A procession of black waiters in white gloves lifted the plates with reverence, like relics from a holy kitchen. A final breath, and they were gone — gliding toward the dining room's velvet and glass battlefield, where money ate money, and I watched knowing nothing would ever be that perfect again. But the ritual wasn't done.

At the table, with the guests poised like high priests before a sacrifice, the waiter lifted the lid with a flourish — steam rising, aromas escaping. Then, with the kind of seriousness reserved for last rites, he poured the veal jus. Not a splash — a controlled stream, glistening, deep, and reduced to velvet. It traced the meat, pooled into the mash trenches, glided across porcelain.

Now it was complete.

The wines? Les Nuages Sauvignon Blanc 2014 — a Loire whisper, light and acidic like the compliments passed between women who hate each other. A £9 bottle dressed up for £90 service. Why French? This was Ascot, for Christ's sake — couldn't they pour a decent Sussex white and pretend to care about supporting British soil?

Syrah Domaine La Croix Belle 2014 — bold, peppery, and forgettable. The kind of wine chosen by a committee that's never seen a vineyard. And then, of course, the Bollinger Rosé. The crowd pleaser. The safe bet. When the corks popped, the room snapped to attention—like a starting gun at a race no one wanted to lose.

It wasn't really a party until someone drenched a £30 bottle of Bollinger Rosé all over a fragile fascinator, the poor thing wilting like a houseplant in the desert. The culprit? Laughing like they'd just made a charitable donation—because nothing says "high society" like wasting champagne on millinery.

After the dessert — Orange and Passionfruit Bavarois, very delicate. The room shifted. Tipsy cheer turned to betting aggression. I slipped out the back with a half-glass of Bollinger Rosé, still cold, still smug. I leaned against the wall, watching the day bruise into late afternoon, and thought about the real cost of luxury. From where I stood it was obvious — the wealth in that room didn't come from clever trades. It came from extraction, plain and simple.

The plates were spotless, the wine endless, and yet,

somewhere far off, an entire continent was still being billed for the party. Gold, diamonds, oil, rubber, souls—dug up, bagged, shipped off in crates marked "civilization." Empire wore a dinner jacket. The Brits showed up first. The French brought menus. But while they cheered, I watched. And while they toasted, I remembered.

Africa.

Not a continent—an open vein. Feeding this theatre. Exporting. Cobalt, coltan, gold, uranium—everything you need to run an iPhone, a war, or a goddamn 5-star menu in Mayfair.

Congo is gutted so Silicon Valley can tweet about sustainability. Niger glows in the dark so France can keep the lights on. Meanwhile, kids dig for lithium with hands that should be holding crayons. They call them developing nations, like poverty is a personal failing. Like poverty is a personal failing! Really.

Like colonization was a speed bump—not a 400-year jackhammer that left the continent gasping. It's not developing. It's recovering—from theft, trauma, and every pair of leather shoes ever bought in London.

One of them asked where I learned to cook like this. I almost answered: "Where everything came at someone else's cost."

But I just smiled. In this business, chefs don't think. But I was—smiling and thinking anyway.

Tell that to the Aboriginal mothers whose children were taken by Crown-sanctioned policy. Or to the millions who starved in Bengal while Churchill rerouted grain to feed empire and war.

Or to the Kenyans, bound and beaten in colonial camps under Queen Elizabeth's early reign—when silence reigned louder than justice. Ceremonial? Ceremonial doesn't run death camps, deny rice, or erase generations. Ceremonial doesn't bleed continents for profit.

And France? Not far behind. They brought haute cuisine and formality, but the act was the same. Took everything but the dust. Meanwhile, the British Royal Family sits on more land than God, sipping Earl Grey from diamond-studded cups, telling the world they're just ceremonial.

I smiled as I stood in their palace of polite plunder, wearing courtesy like a rented costume, tailored for their comfort. Fafa, the fire maker. You see, I'm not impressed. So yeah, I serve. I smile. But I'm not here to worship. I'm just robbing the robbers blind—with clarified butter and a fake grin.

Reparations, served à la carte.

The day was flawless. Not because I'm rich. Not because I "made it." But because, for once, the kitchen gods actually clapped.

And then I went home — knives still sharp, rent still due, kids still hungry.

So you can close this book if you want. File it away under "things I once read", right next to that cookbook you swore you'd use and the self-help manual that didn't. Let the dust settle and pat yourself on the back for "having read something."

But out there, the world keeps moving — and honestly, the less we pay attention, the happier we are.

Out in the Sahara, a goat circles a dead tree, kicking at the sand for something to eat, as if shade might suddenly grow back. In Hungary, the streets are calm, the church bells still ring, and old women walk home from church with bread under their arms like nothing in the world has changed. In New York, someone's selling a Rolex that isn't, someone's crying on the subway, and someone's eating a hot dog at 4 a.m. and calling it dinner. In London, some rich man is congratulating himself for surviving another quarter without paying taxes. Then there's Africa, where people never got a single opportunity — and plenty who've stopped looking. They walk, or cram into rusted buses, drifting without a plan, unsure how they'll make it through tomorrow.

And yet, in all these places — the rich, the poor, the calm, the frantic — life happens. Somewhere right now, there's a line cook swearing at a pan, a waiter is making promises the kitchen can't keep, and a lunatic at the pass holding it all together with spit and adrenaline.

The night's still young. And when it's over, we'll all answer to the same God — so you'd better make the story you hand Him worth hearing.

Because there's still no fucking money in cooking. Just stories like this one. And at least, unlike the Chateaubriand, mine's not for sale.

Liked it? Great.

— now leave a tip!

Publisher & Author
László Szűcs
Email: cheflaszlo@gmail.com

Printed by
Pannónia Nyomda Kft.
1139 Budapest, Frangepán utca 16.
www.pannonianyomda.hu

Cover Design
Katalin Kelemen (aka Kóci) — professional artist, part-time sanity keeper.

Written in
Front of Sainsbury's Local, Peacehaven, England

and

Nágocs, Somogy Megye, Hungary — powered by bad coffee, good bread, and the occasional swearing fit.

Typography & Printing
Printed on 80 g Holmen Cream paper with perfect binding — because cheap paper makes your words look cheap.

First Edition – 2025

ISBN 978-615-02-4406-8

© 2025 László Szűcs. All rights reserved.
No part of this publication may be reproduced, stored, or transmitted in any form or by any means without prior written permission from the author — unless you're making a sandwich on it, in which case, send me a picture.

If you actually read the colophon, you're my kind of reader.